THE EXPLORER'S BIBLE

Volume 1: From Creation to the Exodus

BY SCOTT E. BLUMENTHAL

Behrman House Publishers

www.behrmanhouse.com

Copyright © 2006 Behrman House, Inc.
Published by Behrman House, Inc.
Springfield, NJ 07081
www.behrmanhouse.com

BOOK AND COVER DESIGN:	Howard Levy/Red Rooster Group
STORY ILLUSTRATION:	Risa Towbin Aqua
ACTIVITY ILLUSTRATION:	Bot Roda/AA Reps
ICON ILLUSTRATION:	Jim Steck
EDITORIAL COMMITTEE:	Bette Birnbaum, Martin S. Cohen,
	Dina Maiben, Hillary Zana

The publisher and author gratefully acknowledge the following sources of photographs and graphic images: **Peter Beck/Corbis** cover, 50; **Shirley Berger** 42; **Biblical Archaeological Society** 143; **Scott E. Blumenthal** 10; **Corbis** 35; **Creative Image** 14, 66; **Tim David/Corbis** 84; **Gustave Doré** 99; **Randy Faris/Corbis** 136; **Gila Gevirtz** 72; **The Granger Collection, New York** 63; **Julie Habel/Corbis** 100; **Hulton-Deutsch Collection/Corbis** 27; **A. Inden/zefa/Corbis** 28; **Israelimages/Miki Koren** 46; **Saul H. Landa/Judaic Images** 118; **Howard Levy** 18, 35, 124; **Chris Lisle/Corbis** 114; **Richard Lobell** 36, 108, 128; **Mika/zefa/Corbis** 22; **Aladin Abdel Naby/Reuters/Corbis** 153; **Jose Luis Pelaez, Inc./Corbis** 74; **Israelimages/Tsur Pelly** 56; **Photocuisine/Corbis** 78; **Reuters/Corbis** 58; **Ted Spiegel/Corbis** 90; **Ginny Twersky** 146; **David Wall/OzImages** 32; **Vicki L. Weber** 92; **M. Yablonsky** 154

Library of Congress Cataloging-in-Publication Data

Blumenthal, Scott.
  The explorer's Bible/by Scott E. Blumenthal.
    p. cm.
  Contents: v. 1. From creation to the Exodus
  ISBN-13: 978-0-87441-792-0 (v. 1)
  1. Bible. O.T.—Textbooks. 2. Bible. O.T.—Juvenile literature. 3. Bible. O.T.—Commentaries. 4. Jewish religious education of children. I. Title.

  BS1194.B58 2006
  221.9'505—dc22

                                                                          2006003163

To my beloved grandmother,
Hannah Krakower

And to my mentor and dear colleague,
Gila Gevirtz,
the true Midrash Maker

Contents

Introduction

The Bible is the story of the Jewish people. But it is also *your* story. It is not only the source of Jewish tradition, values, and belief, but also of guidance as you live your life, go to school, and grow up. It allows you to explore who you are and how to become the best possible you.

And now, here's the story of how *The Explorer's Bible* was born…

Did someone say *time?* I'll be the guide back in time to meet the heroes of the Bible and to witness their most dramatic moments. You have my word.

TIME TRAVELER

WORD WIZARD

Did someone say *word?* I'll be the guide to Hebrew words and phrases. We'll find keys to the Bible's meaning and create new keys, called *midrash*.

Did someone say *midrash?* I'll be the guide to understanding the Bible. What was Abraham like at your age, you may ask? The Bible doesn't tell us. So our sages created possible answers called *midrash*— usually stories with lessons.

MIDRASH MAKER

And what should *we* do? There is so much to discover.

Yes—and each student can make a different discovery in each story.

Let's choose one lesson from each chapter. Something that students can use in their everyday lives. Then we'll see what the students think.

Happy exploring!

Well, what are we waiting for?

CHAPTER 1

The Birth of the World

GENESIS 1:1–2:3

וַיְבָ֖רֶךְ
אֱלֹהִים֙ אֶת־י֣וֹם
הַשְּׁבִיעִ֔י
וַיְקַדֵּ֖שׁ אֹת֑וֹ

GENESIS 1:1–5

When God began to create heaven and earth, the earth had no shape and no form. God said, "Let there be light," and there was light. God saw that the light was good. Then God separated the light from the darkness. God called the light Day and the darkness Night. And there was evening and there was morning—the first day.

Imagine the earth with "no shape and no form." What do you think it looked like on the first day?

GENESIS 1:6–8

God said, "Let there be a space between heaven and earth." God called this space Sky. And there was evening and there was morning—the second day.

Why do you think God made fruit trees that produce seeds? What's so important about seeds?

GENESIS 1:9–13

God said, "Let the water below the sky gather into one place, so that dry land appears." And it was so. God called the dry land Earth and the water Seas. God saw that this was good. Then God said, "Let the earth sprout plants and fruit trees that produce seeds." And it was so. God saw that this was good. And there was evening and there was morning—the third day.

In what ways does the sun "rule over the day"? How does the sun affect your day?

Genesis 1:14–19

God said, "Let there be lights in the sky to separate day from night. They will mark the times of day and seasons of the year. They will also serve as lights to shine upon the earth." And it was so. God made two great lights: the larger one to rule over the day and the smaller one to rule over the night, and also the stars. God placed them in the sky and saw that this was good. And there was evening and there was morning—the fourth day.

Genesis 1:20–23

God said, "Let the waters bring forth living creatures." Then God created the great sea creatures, fish of every kind, and birds that fly across the sky. God saw that this was good. God blessed them and said, "Be fruitful and multiply. Fill the water in the seas, and let the birds multiply on the earth." And there was evening and there was morning—the fifth day.

Our sages teach us that God created everything— even bees, fleas, and flies—for a reason.

Only on the sixth day did God say that "it was very good." What was different about the sixth day?

GENESIS 1:24–31

God said, "Let the earth bring forth animals of every kind—tame animals, creeping things, and wild beasts." And it was so. God saw that this was good. Then God said, "Let there be humans, and they will rule over the fish of the sea, the birds of the sky, the animals, and the whole earth." God created humans, male and female, in the image of God. God blessed the humans and said to them, "Be fruitful and multiply. Fill the earth and rule over it. Rule the fish of the sea, the birds of the sky, and all living things that creep on earth." God looked at all that was created and saw that it was very good. And there was evening and there was morning—the sixth day.

In the Image of God
בְּצֶלֶם אֱלֹהִים

WORD WIZARD

Human beings are special among God's creations. Although all the land animals were created on the sixth day, only humans were created *b'tzelem Elohim*— in the image of God. But what does that mean? Do we look like God? Can we make oceans and stars? Not quite. Instead, the rabbis teach us, we are like God in other ways: We can create. We can care for others. We can care for the world.

GENESIS 2:1–3

By the seventh day, the heaven and the earth were finished. God blessed the seventh day and called it holy, because on that day God rested after finishing the work of creation.

Time to Rest

TIME TRAVELER

Flashback! **It is the first Shabbat. You look around at the world that God has created. It is peaceful and complete. In the space below, draw or describe what you see.**

Why do you think it's important to remember this day?

_____

_____

_____

It Was Very Good

On the day you were born, something that had never existed before came into the world: you. There may have been people who looked like you, or sounded like you, or even had the same hobbies and opinions as you. But no one has ever been—or ever will be—exactly like you. You are unique.

When God said to humans, "Fill the earth and rule over it," we became partners with God in improving and protecting the world. Each of us does this in a different way. Together, we can make sure the world is not only *good*, **but** *very good*.

Like a tiny sapling, your contributions to the world will continue to grow every day.

14

Self-Portrait

How will *you* make the world a better place? Choose one of the tools below.
Then draw a picture of yourself using your tool to improve the world.

Now add a caption to your picture. Explain how you are improving the world.

_____

_____

_____

CHAPTER 2

Good and Evil in the Garden of Eden

GENESIS 2:4–3:24

עני והפקידנה עיניה

GENESIS 2:4–15

When God created the world, there was no one to care for it. So God formed a human from the dust of the earth. God blew the breath of life into the human's nostrils, and it became a living being. Then God planted a garden in the land of Eden and placed the human there, to work and tend the earth.

The Hebrew word for "human" is *adam*. From what was *adam* created? From *adamah*, "earth."

GENESIS 2:16–17

There were many beautiful trees in the Garden of Eden. In the middle of the garden stood the Tree of Knowledge of Good and Evil. God said to the human, "You are free to eat from every tree in the garden, except from the Tree of Knowledge of Good and Evil. If you eat from that tree, you will die."

Notice something different? Just before the creation of woman, we hear Adam's name for the first time. Can you think of reasons why?

Genesis 2:18–25

God said, "It is not good to be alone. The human should have a partner." So God formed all the animals of the earth and all the birds of the sky and brought them to the human. Whatever the human called each living thing became its name. But Adam still had no partner. So God cast a deep sleep upon him. While he slept, God took one of his ribs and shaped it into a woman. Adam and the woman were naked, but they were not embarrassed.

Genesis 3:1–3

Then the snake, the most sly of all the animals, said to the woman, "Did God really say that you may not eat from any tree in the garden?" The woman answered, "God said that we may not eat from the Tree of Knowledge of Good and Evil or even touch it, or we will die."

Genesis 3:4–7

The snake said to the woman, "You will not die. God knows that when you eat from it you will be like God, knowing the difference between good and evil." The woman looked at the tree and thought of the knowledge it might bring her. She took a fruit from the tree, and she ate it. She also gave a piece to Adam, and he ate it. Suddenly, their eyes were opened. They noticed that they were naked, and they were embarrassed. They sewed fig leaves together and covered themselves.

Dates

Figs

The Torah does not tell us what kind of fruit hung from the Tree of Knowledge of Good and Evil. Our sages believed that they were either dates or figs.

Repairing the World

Question
What does it mean to "work and tend" the earth?

Classic Midrash
After finishing the work of creation, God lifted Adam high above the Garden of Eden. "Look at what I have created!" God said. "See how beautiful it is, how excellent! I have created all this for your sake, and for the sake of those who come after you. Think about what I have said, and be careful not to destroy My world. For if you do, there will be no one to repair it after you." (Kohelet Rabbah 7:13)

> Remember, a midrash is a story with a lesson that helps us understand the Bible.

Your Midrash
The Bible teaches that God created human beings to care for the world. Create a midrash by describing three ways people can protect nature and the environment.

1. _____

_____

_____

2. _____

_____

_____

3. _____

_____

_____

GENESIS 3:8–13

Then they heard the voice of God in the garden. They hid among the trees. God called out to Adam, "Where are you?" Adam answered, "I heard You in the garden, and I was naked, so I hid." And God replied, "Who told you that you were naked? Did you eat of the Tree of Knowledge of Good and Evil?" The man said, "The woman gave me fruit from the tree, and I ate." God said to the woman, "What have you done?" "The snake tricked me, and I ate," the woman replied.

GENESIS 3:14–19

God said to the snake, "Because you did this, you will be the most cursed of all creatures. You will crawl on your belly and eat dust all the days of your life." To the woman God said, "You will suffer great pain when giving birth." To the man God said, "You must now work hard for as long as you live."

GENESIS 3:20–24

Adam named his wife Eve, which means *life*, because she would give life to all people. Then God took animal skins, made clothing for Adam and Eve, and banished them from the garden. God left holy angels and a blazing sword to keep people out of the Garden of Eden forever.

Have you ever wanted to blame someone else for something you did? What did you decide to do? How did you feel afterward?

God punished Adam and Eve, but at the same time God was kind, making sure they had clothing before going out into the world.

The Biblo-Chat 3000

Flashback! **You're in the Garden of Eden. You've taken the Biblo-Chat 3000, a computer that sends messages between the past and the present. Help us learn more about Adam and Eve by filling in the blank spaces below.**

TimeTraveler: *Eve, how did you feel when you heard God's voice in the garden?*
FirstGirl:

TimeTraveler: *Both of you ate from the tree. Adam, why did you blame Eve for what you did?*
FirstGuy:

TimeTraveler: *Adam and Eve, what did you learn from your experience?*
FirstGirl:

FirstGuy:

A New World

At first, Adam and Eve were like little children. God, like a parent, provided the things they needed: food, a safe home, even a friend so they were not lonely. It was a world without choices. But once they ate from the Tree of Knowledge of Good and Evil, "their eyes were opened." Life would never be the same.

Once they ate from the Tree of Knowledge of Good and Evil, Adam and Eve were no longer like little children. Just like you, they would work hard, feel pain, and even make mistakes. Just like you, they would make tough choices. Just like you, they would face the challenges of growing up.

We make choices every day. Some are less important than others but can feel just as hard to make.

The Chewy Choice Chart

Imagine that you're going on a field trip to the zoo. You have two lunch options: take lunch from home, or use your own money to buy lunch at the zoo.

In the chart below, choose an option—A or B. Circle the specific lunch you choose. Then answer the questions at the bottom of the page.

A. Take lunch from home

B. Buy lunch at the zoo

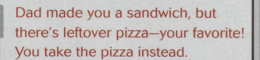

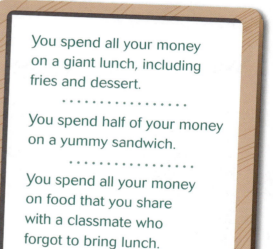

Dad made you a sandwich, but there's leftover pizza—your favorite! You take the pizza instead.

You make a veggie sandwich. You're not excited about it, but you know it's good for you.

You take a big piece of cake. You know that it's not a healthy meal—but it's soooo good.

You spend all your money on a giant lunch, including fries and dessert.
. . . .
You spend half of your money on a yummy sandwich.
. . . .
You spend all your money on food that you share with a classmate who forgot to bring lunch.

Write one thing about your choice that you're happy about.

_____

Write one thing about your choice that you're not happy about.

_____

Imagine that you had the same choices for a whole week. Would you make the same choice for every day? Please explain.

_____

_____

CHAPTER 3

My Brother's Keeper

GENESIS 4:1–15

ויחר
לקין מאד
ויפלו פניו

GENESIS 4:1–5

Adam and Eve had two sons—Cain and Abel. Abel became a shepherd, and Cain became a farmer. One day, Cain brought some fruit that he had grown as an offering to God. Abel brought the finest of his firstborn sheep. God accepted Abel's sheep but not Cain's fruit. Seeing that God accepted Abel's sacrifice and not his own, Cain became upset. His face fell.

In the days of Cain and Abel, people brought animals and food to God as gifts.

GENESIS 4:8–9

One day, when they were in the field, Cain spoke to his brother Abel. Then Cain attacked his brother and killed him. God said to Cain, "Where is your brother Abel?" Cain replied, "How should I know? Am I my brother's keeper?"

Does God's question sound familiar? In the Garden of Eden God asked Adam, "Where are you?" Why do you think God asked Adam and Cain these questions?

25

Cain's Name
קַיִן

WORD WIZARD

In the Torah, people's names often tell us something about them. We know that "Eve" means *life* and that "Adam" means *human*. Later we'll learn that "Abraham" means *father of nations* and "Isaac" means *laughter*. Cain's name means *I got.* But why?

Both Abel and Cain brought sacrifices to God. Abel brought the "finest of his firstborn sheep." He gave the best that he could. But Cain brought simply "some fruit that he had grown." He gave less than his best. Cain was a person who loved to get, but not to give.

Have you ever asked a question to which you already knew the answer? If so, why?

Genesis 4:10–12

Then God said, "What have you done? Your brother's blood is calling out to Me from the ground! You, who have shed blood with your own hands, will be cursed. If you plant seeds, nothing will grow from them. You will become a wanderer on the earth."

Genesis 4:13–15

Then Cain said to God, "My punishment is too great to bear. But now, since I must become a wanderer on earth, anyone who meets me may kill me!" God said to him, "I promise, whoever kills you will be punished seven times over." And God put a mark on Cain so that no one would kill him.

Say What?

The first five books of the Bible are called the Torah. In *The Explorer's Bible*, we'll use both words: Bible and Torah.

Question

What did Cain say to Abel? The Torah doesn't tell us!

Classic Midrash

Cain said to his brother, "Come, let us divide the world." Abel agreed. "Good," said Cain. "You take the animals, and I will take the land." Again, Abel agreed. Later, while Abel was tending his sheep, Cain said to his brother, "You are on my land." Abel replied, "The wool you are wearing comes from my sheep!" Cain said, "Get off my land!" Abel said, "Give me back my wool!" Then Cain attacked his brother Abel and killed him. (B'reisheet Rabbah 22:7)

Your Midrash

What do *you* think Cain might have said?

_____

_____

_____

What do you think Cain *should* have said
that might have produced a better result?

_____

_____

_____

_____

_____

Many important people in the Bible—including Abraham, Isaac, Jacob, and Moses—were shepherds.

The First Question

The story of Cain and Abel contains many "firsts": the first children, the first sacrifices to God, the first jealousy, and the first murder. It also contains the first question to God: "Am I my brother's keeper?"

You'll find that the Torah answers Cain's question again and again:

- When Abraham hears that the people of Sodom and Gomorrah are in danger, he haggles with God to spare their lives.

- When Abraham's servant Eliezer is thirsty, Rebecca draws water not only for him but for his camels as well.

- When Moses sees an Egyptian taskmaster beating a Hebrew slave, he comes to the slave's rescue.

Judaism's answer to the question, "Am I my brother's keeper?" is clear: YES. We are all responsible for one another.

When we care for others, we learn to share and to give of ourselves.

IT'S A KEEPER!

Circle the seven words below that describe someone who is a "brother's keeper." Then find those words inside the word search.

KIND   MEAN   HELPING   RUDE

UNCARING   PATIENT   FRIENDLY   SELFISH

HONEST   SHARING   HURTFUL   GENEROUS

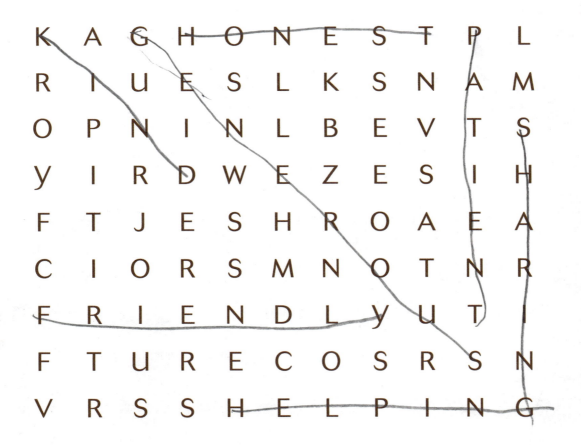

```
K A G H O N E S T P L
R I U E S L K S N A M
O P N I N L B E V T S
Y I R D W E Z E S I H
F T J E S H R O A E A
C I O R S M N O T N R
F R I E N D L Y U T I
F T U R E C O S R S N
V R S S H E L P I N G
```

CHAPTER 4

The Man Who Walked with God

GENESIS 6:5–9:17

GENESIS 6:5–9

God saw that people were treating one another badly. All they did was plan wicked deeds all day long. God said, "I will wipe out the humans that I created. I wish that I had never made them!" But in that wicked time there was one man, Noah, who was a *tzaddik*—a righteous person. Noah walked with God.

What *do* you think it means to "walk with God"? What kind of a person "walks with God"?

GENESIS 6:14–22

God said to Noah, "Make an ark of cedar wood and seal it with tar. It should have many rooms, a window at the top, and a door on its side. I am about to flood the earth, and everything on earth will die. But I will make a covenant with you, Noah. You and your family will enter the ark, along with two of each animal—one male and one female. Collect food for yourselves and for the animals and store it away." And Noah did as God commanded.

A covenant is an agreement or promise.

31

Genesis 7:6–23

When Noah was six hundred years old, he brought his family and animals of every kind into the ark. Seven days later, the sky burst open. Rain fell on the earth for forty days and forty nights. The waters rose so high that even the tallest mountains were covered. All the animals and all the humans on earth died. Only Noah and those with him in the ark remained safe.

Genesis 7:24–8:9

After forty days, God caused a wind to blow across the earth, and the rain stopped. After the flood had been on the earth one hundred and fifty days, the waters began to dry up. The ark came to rest in the mountains of Ararat. Noah opened the window of the ark and sent out a raven. The raven flew around, searching for a place to land. When the raven did not return, Noah sent out a dove. But the dove could not find a resting place and returned to the ark.

Getting to Noah You

TIME TRAVELER

Flashback! **You are Noah, and it is 100 years after the flood. Your many grandchildren have lots of questions about your days on the ark. Answer their questions about your experiences, so they can teach *their* grandchildren.**

How did you react when God told you about the flood?

I went insane

What was hardest about being on the ark for so long?

you get seasick

What was the most fun?

builring the ark and anic

The Bird of Peace

MIDRASH MAKER

Question
Why did Noah choose the dove to be his messenger?

Classic Midrash
The animals heard a rumor: Noah would take only his favorite animals with him on the ark. So they came to Noah to boast about themselves. The lion roared, "I am the strongest of the beasts. I must be saved." The elephant blared, "But I am the largest." "But I give eggs," clucked the hen.

Noah noticed the dove sitting quietly on a branch. "Why are you silent, little dove?" "I don't think of myself as better than the others," cooed the dove. "Each of us has something the others do not, something given to us by God." "The dove is right," Noah said. "That is why all of you shall come into the ark. But because the dove was modest, I choose it to be my messenger." (Isaac Bashevis Singer, "Why Noah Chose the Dove")

Your Midrash
Complete the story below to create your own midrash.

One day on the ark, Noah overheard a rabbit and giraffe arguing. "We are too different to be friends," said the giraffe. "I agree," said the rabbit. Then the dove spoke up. "It is true that you are different. But here is why you should be friends:

because they agree

GENESIS 8:10–14

After seven days, Noah again sent out the dove. This time, the dove returned with an olive leaf in its beak. Seeing this, Noah knew that the earth was beginning to dry. Noah waited another seven days and sent the dove again. This time, the dove did not return. The earth was finally dry.

The olive leaf showed Noah that the waters had gone down far enough for the tops of trees to appear.

GENESIS 8:15–9:6

Then God said to Noah, "Come out of the ark with your family. Bring every living thing that is with you—the birds, the animals, and all the creeping things. Let them be fruitful and multiply on the earth." Then God blessed Noah and his family and said, "You may eat animals and plants, but you may not eat animals that are still alive. And you may not kill people, for they are created in the image of God."

"Created in the image of God"? We've heard that before, when God first formed humans.

GENESIS 9:8–17

Then God said, "I will establish My covenant with you and with those who come after you, and with every living creature, forever. I promise never again to destroy the earth. I have placed a rainbow in the clouds. This is the sign of the covenant between Me and you."

Why do you think God chose a rainbow as the sign of the covenant?

Standing His Ground

Our sages told this story: While Noah built the ark, his neighbors stood around and laughed. "What are you *doing?*" they asked. "God sees that people do wicked deeds all the time," Noah answered. "Soon God will bring a flood to destroy the world." Noah hoped that his neighbors would hear his words and change their wicked ways. Then God would not have to destroy the world after all. But even when Noah and his family boarded the ark, his neighbors still just stood around and laughed.

When everyone around us is behaving poorly, it can be difficult to do what is right. But Noah knew better. Noah showed kindness and respect to others, even though those around him did not. Perhaps that is why the Torah calls him a *tzaddik*, a "righteous person." Noah stood his ground. He did what he knew was right.

The Bible tells us that Noah was a tzaddik, *a "righteous person." The word* tzaddik *is related to the word* tzedakah, *"righteous giving."*

Finding Courage

It takes courage to do what is right—especially if people around you are behaving poorly. Help Noah find his way through the maze to find the courage he needs.

COURAGE

CHAPTER 5

The Impossible Tower

GENESIS 11:1–9

GENESIS 11:1–4

Long ago, everyone on earth spoke the same language. Like nomads, they moved from place to place. One day, they came to a valley in the land of Shinar and settled there. Before long, the people said to one another, "Come, let us take clay from the ground, make it into bricks, and bake them until they are hard. We will build ourselves a tower with its top in the heavens. If we do, we will make a name for ourselves, and people will always remember us."

What are some actions we can take to "make a name for ourselves" in a good way? In a bad way?

GENESIS 11:5–7

God came down and saw the tower that the people had built. "If they remain one people, with one language," God said, "then this is only the beginning of what they will be able to do. Soon they will do anything they wish. I will confuse their language, so that they will not be able to understand one another."

Why do you think God became angry with the builders?

The Shamayim Connection

There	שָׁם
Heaven	שָׁמַיִם
Name	שֵׁם

When we translate the Bible from Hebrew to English (or French or Chinese or Swahili), we sometimes miss clues to understanding its meaning. In this story we find three Hebrew words—*sham*, *shamayim*, and *shem*—that sound alike and provide clues to the story's meaning.

Sham means "there," the place where the builders built. *Shamayim* means "heavens" or "sky," the place the builders wanted to reach. What was their reason for climbing from *sham* to *shamayim*? To make themselves a *shem*, a "name" that would be remembered forever. But instead, the Torah teaches us, the builders were scattered across the earth. Now the distance between *sham* and *shamayim* is even greater than before!

The English word *babble* means "confused speech."

GENESIS 11:8–9

So God divided the language of the builders into many languages. That is why the place was called Babel, because when people spoke, their neighbors heard only babble. The people stopped building the tower, and God scattered them over the face of the earth.

Say What?

Time Traveler

Flashback! **God has divided a single language into many. Without understanding one another's words, it's too hard to continue building the tower. See for yourself. Tell the story of the Tower of Babel using pictures only. No letters allowed!**

In 1563, Pieter Bruegher the Elder painted what he thought the Tower of Babel might have looked like.

Reaching Great Heights

WISDOM WEAVERS

Have you ever believed, even for a moment, that you could flap your arms and fly? We all sometimes want to do what is impossible, even though we know that we'll fall short—or fall on our faces.

The builders of the Tower of Babel wanted to build a tower into the heavens. They wanted it so badly that they convinced themselves they could do it. But they wanted what they could not have. They wanted the impossible.

Judaism teaches us not to focus on what is impossible. We should be ambitious and strive to accomplish great things, but we should be mindful of what is within our control and what is not. Only then can we truly do the best that we possibly can— and be the best that we can possibly be.

Once we accept ourselves for who we are, we can climb mountains.

Which Is Which?

Some things we can do by ourselves, some things require a community, and some things are just impossible! It's important to know which is which. Connect each activity to the category it best fits.

Now write or draw your own activity for each category:

put out a forest fire

juggle three buses

write a book

turn a cat into a chicken

build a synagogue

I can do it alone.

We can do it together.

It's impossible!

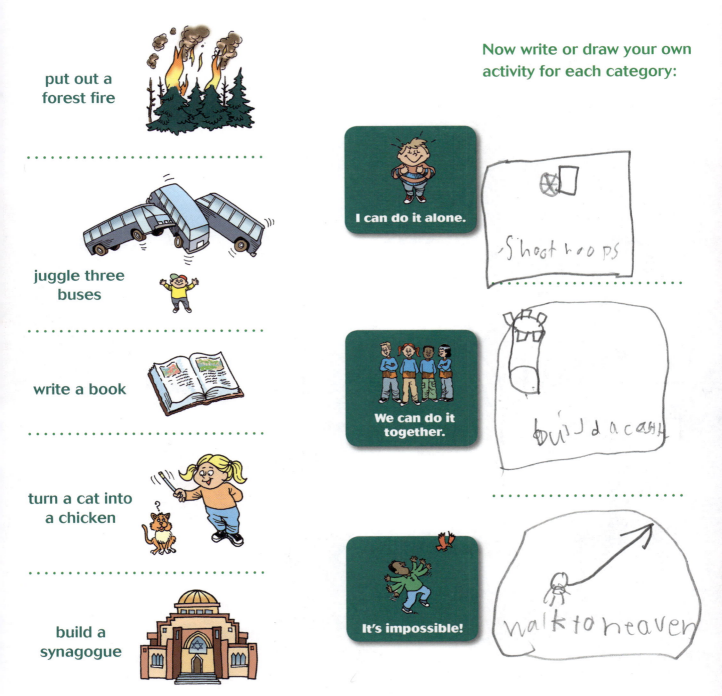

Shoot hoops

build a car

walk to heaven

43

CHAPTER 6

Abraham Finds His Way

GENESIS 11:26–21:6

Genesis 11:26–12:7

In the city of Haran lived Abram, his wife Sarai, and his nephew Lot. One day, God said to Abram, "Leave your country, your homeland, and go to the land that I will show you. I will make of you a great nation, and I will bless you." Abram, along with Sarai and Lot, took everything they owned and set out for the land of Canaan. Abram was seventy-five years old when he left Haran. When they arrived in Canaan, God appeared to Abram and said, "This land that I give you now will belong to your descendants forever."

What does it feel like to go to a strange new place for the first time?

45

Think of a time when things were difficult because of limited space or time. How did you resolve the problem?

Genesis 13:1–7

In time, Abram and Lot acquired many possessions, including cattle, donkeys, and camels. Soon, there wasn't enough land to support both of them and their animals. The herdsmen who cared for Abram's cattle and those who cared for Lot's cattle began to argue over the land.

Genesis 13:8–16

Abram said to Lot, "We should not argue, for we are family. Look at all the land before us. Let us part from one another. If you go north, I will go south. If you go south, I will go north." Abram and Lot said goodbye. Abram remained where he was, and Lot settled near the city of Sodom. Then God said to Abram, "Look to the north and south, to the east and west. All the land that you see, I give to you and to your descendants forever. Your descendants will be like the specks of dust on the earth—too many to count."

Abram and Sarai's long journey led them through the Negev, in the south of modern-day Israel.

Like Specks of Dust on the Earth

כַּעֲפַר הָאָרֶץ

God promised Abram that his descendants would be *ka'afar ha'aretz*, "like the specks of dust on the earth." Now that's a lot of descendants. The Torah compares the Jewish people to specks of dust, our sages taught, for three reasons:

- There are so many specks of dust on the earth that no one can count them. One day, the Jewish people will be too many to count.

- There will be specks of dust on earth forever. Likewise, the Jewish people will live forever.

- There is dust everywhere on earth. So, too, the Jewish people will live throughout the world.

(adapted from B'reisheet Rabbah 41:9)

GENESIS 17:1–18:16

When Abram was ninety-nine years old, God appeared to him and said, "Your name will no longer be Abram, but Abraham—the father of nations. Sarai will no longer be Sarai, but Sarah. She will be the mother of nations. I will bless her, and she will have a son." Abraham fell to the ground and laughed. He said to himself, "How can a child be born to a man who is one hundred years old, or to a woman who is ninety?" God said, "Sarah will bear a son at this time next year. I will keep my covenant with him and his descendants forever."

One day, while sitting at the entrance of his tent, Abraham looked up and saw three men coming toward him. Abraham ran to greet them. He bowed to the ground and said, "My lords, please stay. I will have water and food brought over. Please, relax under the tree." Abraham hurried into the tent to Sarah, who prepared cakes of the finest flour. Abraham ran to his herd and chose a calf to serve to his guests. Then Abraham set the meal before them. When the guests were finished, Abraham walked with them, toward Sodom, to send them off.

GENESIS 21:1–6

Some time later, Sarah and Abraham had a son, just as God had promised. "Everyone who hears that I had a son in my old age will laugh with me," Sarah said. So they named him "Isaac," meaning *laughter*.

Abraham practiced the Jewish value of hachnasat orḥim, welcoming guests. How do you feel when you are greeted warmly by a host?

Young Abraham

Question

The story of Abraham begins when he is seventy-five years old. So what was he like as a young person? Why did God choose him?

Classic Midrash

Abram's father, Teraḥ, was an idol-maker who sold carved images of stone. One day, Teraḥ left Abram to take care of the shop. Abram saw the idols around him, and he picked up an ax.

When Teraḥ returned, he found the shop littered with smashed pieces of stone. Only one large idol remained whole. "Who has done this?" cried Teraḥ. "The big god took your ax and killed them all," replied Abram. Teraḥ said, "Abram, you are mocking me! You know that idols can't move." Then Abram said, "Father, let your ears hear what your tongue speaks." (B'reisheet Rabbah 38:13)

Your Midrash

Create your own midrash that explains why God chose Abraham. Begin with this story starter:

One day, when Abram was twelve years old, he _____

_____

_____

_____

_____

_____

Finding Direction

A compass helps us to find our way. If we want to know which direction to go in the world, whether we're hiking through the woods or sailing to Spain, a compass is the perfect tool. If we want to know which direction to go in our lives, we use a different kind of compass: a moral compass. Each of us has a moral compass that helps us make good decisions.

When Lot needed more space for his herd, Abram's moral compass guided him to share. When the three guests came to Abram's tent, Abram's moral compass guided him to be welcoming. Later, Abram's moral compass will guide him to speak up for what he believes is right. Abram's moral compass guided him every step of the way.

We can't expect to always be right, but if we have faith in our moral compass, we can head in the right direction.

And the Winner Is...

Think of someone you know who has a strong moral compass—someone who is honest and kind. Give that person a Moral Compass Award. Explain what that person does that is honest and kind. Then decorate the award.

Moral Compass Award

This award goes to

_____

because

_____

_____

_____

_____

SEAL OF APPROVAL

CHAPTER 7

Abraham Speaks Up

GENESIS 18:20–19:29

וַיֹּאמֶר
יְהֹוָה
בַּעֲבוּרָם

GENESIS 18:20–21

God said, "I have heard the wickedness of Sodom and Gomorrah. Their sins are great. I will go down to see what they have done, to see if what I hear is true. If it is true, I will destroy the cities."

GENESIS 18:23–26

Abraham came before God and said, "Will You destroy the innocent along with the guilty? What if there are fifty innocent people in the city? Would You destroy the city and not forgive it for the sake of fifty innocent people? It is not right to do such a thing. Shouldn't the Judge of all the earth act justly?" God answered, "If I find fifty innocent people in Sodom, I will forgive the whole city for their sake."

The Torah does not describe the sins of Sodom and Gomorrah. According to midrash, the citizens cheated, lied, and encouraged one another to do wicked things.

This is the first time that anyone in the Torah has challenged God in this way. Why do you think Abraham was so bold?

53

Abraham and Noah each heard that something terrible was about to happen. How were their reactions different? How were they the same?

GENESIS 18:27–32

But Abraham said, "I am just a human being, nothing but dust and ashes, but please permit me to speak. What if You look for fifty innocent people, but are lacking only five?" And God answered, "I will not destroy the city if I find forty-five innocent people there." But Abraham continued. "Please do not be angry if I go on," he said. "What if thirty are found there?" And God answered, "I will not do it if I find thirty." But Abraham said, "I dare once again to speak: What

I Will Go Down to See

אֵרֲדָה־נָּא וְאֶרְאֶה

Wait a second. Why would God say, "I will go down to see" what was happening in Sodom? Couldn't God have seen the city from anywhere?

Have you ever been blamed for something you didn't do? Or blamed someone else based on what you *heard* or *supposed*? Sometimes we accuse others without good reason. When God says, *eiradah-na v'ereh*, "I will go down to see," the Torah teaches us an important lesson: We should not judge others based on what *may* be true. We should see for ourselves, we should know for ourselves, and we should judge for ourselves.

if twenty are found there?" And God answered, "I will not destroy it, for the sake of the twenty." And Abraham said, "Please do not be angry if I speak one last time: What if ten are found there?" And God answered, "I will not destroy the city, for the sake of the ten."

GENESIS 19:1–5

That evening, two visitors arrived in Sodom. Lot rose to greet them and said, "Friends, please, spend the night here." Lot prepared a feast for them, and they ate. They had not yet gone to sleep when all the men of Sodom, young and old, gathered around Lot's house. They shouted to Lot, "Where are the strangers who came to you tonight? Bring them out to us, so that we may abuse them! You know that this is our custom with visitors."

The Torah tells us that "all the men of Sodom" came to attack Lot's guests. This did not help Abraham, who hoped to find ten good people—there was hardly a single one!

GENESIS 19:6–11

Lot went out to the men and said, "I beg you, do not do this wicked thing." But the men of Sodom said, "Lot came here as a stranger, and already he acts as though he is in charge." Then they said to Lot, "Now we will punish you worse than them!" And they moved forward to grab Lot. But the visitors quickly pulled Lot inside and shut the door. The crowd at the door was struck with a blinding light, so bright that they could not find the entrance.

GENESIS 19:15-26

Just before dawn, the visitors said to Lot, "Take your family and run for your lives. Hurry, get out of this city, for God is about to destroy it. Do not look back, or you will die!" Lot did as the visitors said. Then, as the sun rose, God rained down fire, destroying Sodom and Gomorrah and everyone who lived there. From outside the city, Lot's wife looked back—and she turned into a pillar of salt.

GENESIS 19:27-29

The next morning, Abraham rushed to the edge of a cliff and looked upon Sodom and Gomorrah. He saw smoke rising from the cities. God had destroyed them. But God had remembered Abraham and saved Lot and his daughters.

The cities of Sodom and Gomorrah are believed to have been near the Dead Sea, a lake so salty that pillars of salt will sometimes emerge from it.

Decisions, Decisions!

Flashback! **You are a member of Lot's family. You've just been told that you must leave Sodom—quickly! You may take only three items with you. From the list below, circle the three items you consider most important. Then explain the reason for each of your choices.**

your favorite toy

a vase you had made for your mother (it took weeks to make!)

a loaf of bread (you're hungry already!)

your warm blanket (it gets cold at night)

a necklace that your best friend made for you

your sister's sandals (she forgot them)

1. Bread

2. blanket

3. sandles

57

Speak Up!

When Abraham heard the news about Sodom and Gomorrah, he could have chosen to do nothing. But Abraham believed that it was wrong for God to destroy any innocent people who may have been living in the cities. So he chose to speak up for what he believed. By questioning God, Abraham teaches us to speak up for what we believe is right—and to do so in an appropriate way.

These girls are marching for peace in Israel.
They are standing up for what they believe is right.

BE A HERO!

Look around your classroom—even in school there are opportunities to stand up for what is right. In the classroom below, some students are doing the right thing, some are not. Circle three students who are *not* doing the right thing. For each, explain what you might do or say to make the situation better.

1. writing on desk
2. eating fotatoe
3. Pull hair

CHAPTER 8

The Sacrifice

GENESIS 22:1–13

וַיֵּרָא
הָשָׁה
לְעֹלָה

Genesis 22:1–2

One day, God tested Abraham. "Abraham," God said. Abraham replied, "I am here." God said, "Take your son Isaac, whom you love, and bring him up to the land of Moriah, to the mountain that I will show you, to offer him as a sacrifice."

This famous story is known as the Akedah, the "binding" of Isaac.

Genesis 22:3–5

Early the next morning, Abraham placed a saddle on his donkey and prepared the wood for the sacrifice. Then he set out, along with two servants and his son Isaac. After three days, Abraham looked up and saw a mountain. He said to his servants, "Stay here. The boy and I will go up the mountain. We will worship there and then return to you."

Imagine how Abraham might have felt during those three days of traveling, knowing what he had been told to do.

GENESIS 22:6–8

Abraham took the knife and the flint to start the fire, and the two walked up the mountain together. Then Isaac said to his father Abraham, "Father!" And Abraham answered, "Yes, my son." And Isaac said, "Here is the flint and the wood, but where is the sheep for the sacrifice?" And Abraham said, "God will provide the sheep for the sacrifice, my son." And the two of them walked on together.

I Am Here
הִנֵּנִי

The word *hineni*, "I am here," has a special place in the Bible. When God called upon our ancestors to perform difficult or life-changing tasks, their response was often the same: *hineni*.

- When God called upon Abraham to sacrifice his son, Abraham responded: *hineni*.
- When God called upon Moses to lead the children of Israel out of Egypt, Moses responded: *hineni*.
- When God called upon the prophet Isaiah to deliver a message to the people, Isaiah responded: *hineni*.

With the word *hineni*, our ancestors showed God that they had faith and trust in what was about to happen.

In 1928, diggers in Israel discovered a 1,500-year-old synagogue called Beit Alfa. Inside was a mosaic telling the story of the Akedah.

Of all the stories in the Torah, this may be the hardest to understand. Why did God test Abraham in this way? What does the story teach us? There are no easy answers.

GENESIS 22:9–13

Abraham built an altar and set the wood in place. He bound his son Isaac and laid him on top of the wood. Then Abraham picked up the knife to sacrifice his son. Suddenly, an angel of God called to him from heaven: "Abraham! Abraham!" And Abraham answered, "I am here." The angel said, "Do not hurt the boy, or do anything to him. Now I know that you respect God." When Abraham looked up, he saw a ram caught in a bush by its horns. Abraham took the ram and offered it up as a sacrifice instead of his son.

Searching for Answers

MIDRASH MAKER

Question
Why would God call upon Abraham to perform such a terrible task?

Classic Midrash
Our sages taught: Abraham was confused. He said to God, "But You said, 'Burn your son as a sacrifice.' Then You said, 'Do not hurt the boy.' Why did You change Your mind?" God said, "I did not change My mind at all. I did not say, 'Burn your son as a sacrifice.' I said, '*Bring him up* to offer him as a sacrifice.' I only wanted to test you. I only told you to bring Isaac up. You thought that I wanted you to burn him as a sacrifice. But I never wanted that." (based on Yalkut Me'am Lo'ez)

Your Midrash
Imagine that you are Abraham. It is the evening after you almost sacrificed your son. Write a diary entry that describes your experience. What were you thinking as you approached the mountain? How did you feel when God called your name?

Dear Diary:
You won't believe what happened to me today. _____

_____

_____

_____

_____

_____

_____

_____

The Test of Time

On Rosh Hashanah, we hear the blast of the shofar—the trumpet made from the horn of a ram. It reminds us that the Jewish New Year has arrived. At the same time, it reminds us of the Akedah— the binding of Isaac—when God provided Abraham with a ram to sacrifice instead of his son. It reminds us of the test God gave to Abraham.

The sound of the shofar also reminds us that we, like Abraham, face an important test: to better understand our relationship with God. Thankfully, our test is different from Abraham's. When we give tzedakah, show kindness to our classmates, and respect our parents, we all pass our tests with flying colors.

We blow the shofar—and read the story of the binding of Isaac— on Rosh Hashanah, the Jewish New Year.

Akedah Crossword Puzzle

Complete the crossword puzzle using the clues below.

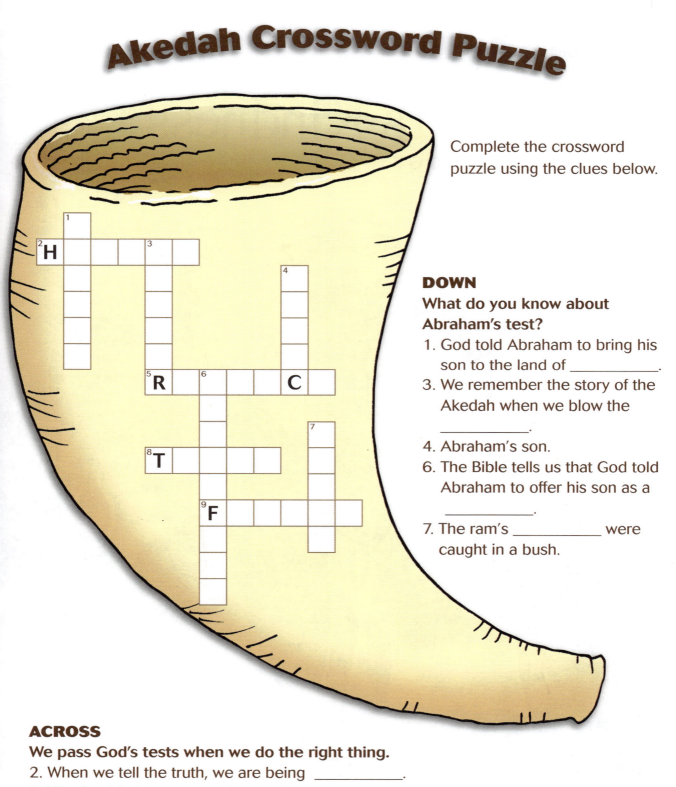

1 [ ]
2 H [ ][ ][ ]   **3** [ ][ ]
4 [ ]
5 R [ ]   **6** [ ][ ]   C [ ][ ]
7
8 T [ ][ ][ ][ ]
9 F [ ][ ][ ][ ]

DOWN
What do you know about Abraham's test?
1. God told Abraham to bring his son to the land of _____.
3. We remember the story of the Akedah when we blow the

   _____.
4. Abraham's son.
6. The Bible tells us that God told Abraham to offer his son as a

   _____.
7. The ram's _____ were caught in a bush.

ACROSS
We pass God's tests when we do the right thing.
2. When we tell the truth, we are being _____.
5. We should always treat other people with _____.
8. We learn important lessons when we study the _____.
9. A good _____ is kind, patient, and trustworthy.

CHAPTER 9

Rebecca's Kindness

GENESIS 23:1–24:67

וַהֲנֵה
רִבְקָה
יֹצֵאת

GENESIS 23:1–19

Sarah lived to be 127 years old. When she died, Abraham cried tears of sorrow. Now, Abraham needed to buy land. He spoke to his neighbors, the Hittite people. "Please sell me a plot of land so I can bury my dead." And the Hittites replied, "You are special in the eyes of God. Please, choose any burial place you wish." So Abraham bought an area of land called Machpelah, which included a cave. Abraham buried Sarah in the cave of Machpelah.

Our sages called Sarah the greatest "woman of honor" in the Bible. In your opinion, what makes someone a person of honor?

GENESIS 24:1–7

Years later, Abraham said to his servant Eliezer, "Go to the land of my birth to find a wife for my son Isaac. Promise me that you will do this." Eliezer replied, "What if the woman does not wish to return with me?" Abraham answered, "God will send an angel before you. The angel will help you find a wife for my son."

Why did Abraham ask Eliezer to make a promise? Why are promises important?

69

Do you think that Eliezer's plan was a good one? Why or why not?

GENESIS 24:10–14

Eliezer took many gifts and ten of Abraham's camels and set out for Abraham's homeland. After many days, he arrived at the city of Nahor. He stopped near a well, so that his camels could drink. The women of the city were drawing water from the well. Eliezer prayed. "God of my master Abraham," he said, "grant me good fortune today. I am standing here as the daughters of the town come out to draw water. I will say, 'Please, lower your jug so that I may drink.' The one who replies, 'Drink, and I will also water your camels' will be the one whom You have chosen for Isaac."

GENESIS 24:15–21

At that moment, along came Rebecca, daughter of Abraham's nephew, carrying a jug on her shoulder. She went down to the well and filled her jug with water. Eliezer said to her, "Please, let me sip a little water from your jug." "Please, sir, drink," she said, and quickly lowered her jug for Eliezer. When he was finished drinking, she said, "I will also draw water for your camels." She ran back to the well and drew water for all his camels. Eliezer stood staring. Could he have already found the right woman?

What an Angel!

Time Traveler

Flashback! You are the angel who helps Eliezer. You watch Rebecca and Eliezer as they talk. Things seem to be going well. Draw what you see. Below your picture, write three words that describe Rebecca.

Derech Eretz   lovely   Beutiful

71

Think of someone you know who is generous and kind. What makes that person special?

GENESIS 24:22–27

When the camels finished drinking, Eliezer gave Rebecca gifts—a gold ring and two gold bracelets. "Please tell me," he said, "Who are you?" "I am Rebecca, the daughter of Bethuel," she replied. "Rebecca, is there room in your father's house for us to spend the night?" "There is plenty of room," she said, "and also straw and feed for your camels." Eliezer said a prayer of thanks to God.

GENESIS 24:28–60

Rebecca ran to tell her family all that had happened. Her brother Laban came out to greet Eliezer at the well. "Come," he said, "I have made the house ready for you and your camels." That evening, Eliezer told Rebecca's family why he had come. Laban and Bethuel took Rebecca aside.

When Rebecca drew water for Eliezer's camels, she taught us the Jewish value of respect for all living creatures.

All His Camels

לְכָל-גְּמַלָּיו

Rebecca drew water for *all* of Eliezer's camels? That's some offer. Eliezer had ten camels with him. Camels require about 25 gallons of water to fill up after a long journey. That's 250 gallons of water for Rebecca to draw from the well! That's a lot of H_2O.

When the Torah tells us about Rebecca's generous act, it includes the words *l'chol g'malav*, "all his camels." In this way, the Torah shows us that Rebecca was not only polite, she was a person of extraordinary generosity.

They asked her, "Will you go with him, to marry this man Isaac?" And Rebecca said, "I will." And they blessed Rebecca.

GENESIS 24:61–67

One evening, while Isaac was walking in the field, he saw camels approaching. Looking out into the field, Rebecca saw Isaac. She asked Eliezer, "Who is that man walking toward us?" He replied, "That is Isaac, my master." Eliezer told Isaac everything that had happened. Soon after, Isaac married Rebecca, who helped Isaac to find comfort even after the death of his mother.

Manners Matter

Human beings have a lot in common with other creatures: We eat, sleep, find food, then eat some more. But only human beings are capable of respectful behavior—such as being polite and using good manners—that sets us apart from our furry and slimy friends. Jewish tradition calls this everyday respect *derech eretz*.

Rebecca understood the importance of *derech eretz*—and she used that understanding to take action. When Eliezer was thirsty, she offered him water. When he needed shelter for the night, she opened her home. She even provided water, food, and shelter for his camels and everyone who was with him. Now that's *derech eretz*.

Being a good listener is an example of derech eretz.

Derech Eretz Way

(for two or more players)

Below is a map of a new street: Derech Eretz Way. Help make the street a great place to live by treating others with kindness and respect.

To walk along the street, flip a coin. If it lands on "heads," move forward one space. If "tails," move forward two spaces. If you land on a DERECH ERETZ ALERT, explain what you would do to help the person you meet. Then write your initials inside the space. The first person to initial four different spaces is the winner!

CHAPTER 10

Twins, Tricks, and Trouble

GENESIS 25:21–27:41

רְבִקָה אֱשֶׁת יִצְחָק

GENESIS 25:21–23

Isaac prayed that he and his wife Rebecca would have a child. God answered his prayers, and Rebecca became pregnant. But Rebecca's pain was so terrible that she too prayed to God. "Two nations are in your womb," God said. "One will be stronger than the other, and the older one will serve the younger."

GENESIS 25:24–28

Finally, the twins were born. The first baby was covered with red hair, so they named him Esau, meaning "hairy." His brother was holding Esau's heel, so they named him Jacob, meaning "heel." When the boys grew up, Esau became a hunter— a man who loved the outdoors. Jacob was a quiet man who liked to stay at home. Because Isaac liked to eat meat from the hunt, his favorite son was Esau. But Rebecca's favorite son was Jacob.

In the Bible, people's names often describe them in some way. What is your Hebrew name? What does it mean?

GENESIS 25:29–34

One day, Jacob was cooking a thick, red lentil stew when Esau returned from a hunt. Esau said to his brother, "Give me some of that red stuff. I'm starving!" Jacob said, "First, you must sell me your birthright." "I'm dying of hunger," Esau replied. "What good is my birthright to me?" But Jacob said, "Promise me first." Esau promised him, and Jacob gave Esau some of the stew. This is how Esau sold his birthright.

A lentil stew like this one might have tempted Esau to sell his birthright.

GENESIS 27:1–4

Many years later, when Isaac was old and he was losing his sight, he called to his older son Esau. "My son," he said. "I am old now, and I may die soon. Take your hunting tools—your quiver and your bow—and go out and hunt for me. Prepare the meat the way I like it and bring it to me. Then I will have the strength to give you my special blessing before I die."

GENESIS 27:5–13

Rebecca had been listening as Isaac spoke. When Esau went out to hunt, as his father had requested, Rebecca said to Jacob, "Listen carefully. Bring me two goats from our flock. I will prepare a meal for your father, just as he likes it. Then you will take it to him, so that he will bless you instead of your brother." Jacob answered, "But my brother Esau is hairy, and my skin is smooth. If my father touches me, he will think I am trying to trick him. Then I will bring upon myself a curse, not a blessing." But Rebecca said, "No, if that happens, the curse will be on *me!*"

Why do you think Rebecca made this plan? How would you have felt if you were Jacob? If you were Isaac? If you were Esau?

What a Deal!

Question
Why did Esau sell his birthright?

Classic Midrash
Our teachers taught: Esau said to Jacob, "Come, give me some of your stew. I am starving!" "I did not prepare it for you," Jacob replied. Esau said, "I'll give you my birthright for the stew." Jacob was shocked. "Your birthright?" "Yes," replied Esau. "Of what use is my birthright? I am a hunter, always close to death. Whatever I get today, I take."

Esau did not think about the future. He was only concerned with today. That is why he sold his birthright for a bowl of lentils.

(B'reisheet Rabbah 63:16, 18)

Your Midrash
What's another reason why Esau might have sold his birthright? Create a midrash of your own by filling in the thoughts of both brothers. Have each brother explain his actions.

Jacob's explanation:

_____
_____
_____
_____
_____
_____

Esau's explanation:

_____
_____
_____
_____
_____
_____

GENESIS 27:14–20

Jacob brought the goats to his mother, and she prepared a meal. Then she covered Jacob's hands and neck with the hairy goat skin. Jacob took the meal to his father. Isaac said, "Which of my sons are you?" Jacob said, "I am Esau, your firstborn. Please sit up and eat the meal I prepared, so that you may give me your special blessing." Isaac said to his son, "How did you return so quickly, my son?" And Jacob said, "Because God was good to me."

Think of three reasons why Isaac might have suspected a trick.

GENESIS 27:21–23

Isaac said to Jacob, "Come closer, so that I may touch your arm, to know whether you are really Esau or not." So Jacob came close to his father. Isaac placed his hand on the goat skin. "The voice is the voice of Jacob," thought Isaac, "but the hands are the hands of Esau." He was doubtful, but because Jacob's arms were hairy like Esau's, Isaac blessed him.

GENESIS 27:30–36

Once Jacob left, Esau returned from his hunt. He too prepared a meal and brought it to his father. "Please," Esau said, "sit up and eat the meal I prepared, so that you may give me your special blessing." But Isaac said, "Who are you?" Esau replied, "I am your son Esau, your firstborn." Isaac began to tremble with fear. "Who was it," he demanded, "that brought me the meal before you came? I blessed him, and with him the blessing must remain!" When Esau heard his father's words, he burst into bitter sobbing. He said to his father, "Bless me too, father!" But Isaac answered, "Your brother tricked me and took away your blessing." Esau said, "First he took my birthright and now he has taken my blessing!"

GENESIS 27:41

Esau hated Jacob because of this. He said to himself, "When my father dies I will mourn for him, and then I will kill my brother Jacob."

Think of the last time in the Torah when one sibling was jealous of another. How did that story end? How do you think *this* story will end?

82

Tricky, Tricky!

Flashback! **There are all sorts of strange conversations in Isaac and Rebecca's home these days. Connect each quote to the *two* people who might have said it.**

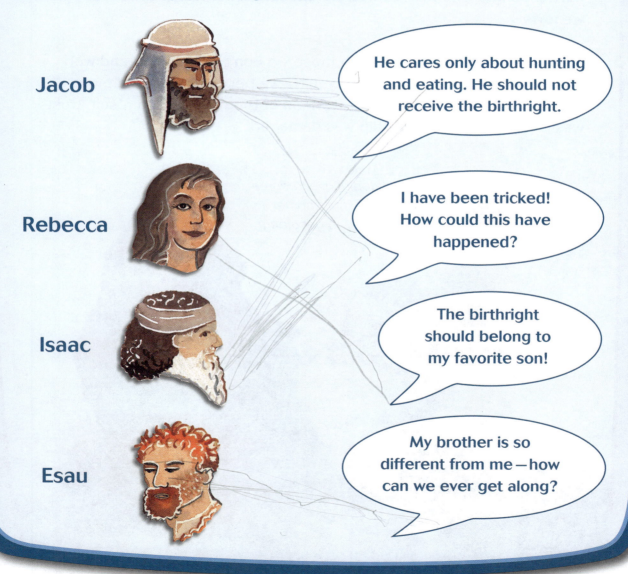

Jacob

Rebecca

Isaac

Esau

He cares only about hunting and eating. He should not receive the birthright.

I have been tricked! How could this have happened?

The birthright should belong to my favorite son!

My brother is so different from me—how can we ever get along?

Agree to Disagree

It's not easy to get along with everyone all of the time. Sometimes we disagree or argue with those whose opinions or beliefs are different from ours. Sometimes we even lose our temper and say hurtful things. When we do this, we can lose a friendship or hurt people we love.

When we learn to get along with those we don't agree with—and work toward settling our disputes peacefully—we become wiser and more mature. Jacob and Esau did not work on getting along. As a result, trust was lost and their relationship was damaged.

We don't have to agree with one another in order to get along.

Spot the Differences

We don't have to agree with one another in order to be great classmates, family members, team members, or friends. In fact, often it's our differences that make us interesting and unique. See for yourself....

Listed below are some of Alex's opinions. Check whether you agree or disagree with Alex.

Alex's Opinions	I Agree	I Disagree
A. Going to the movies is more fun than bowling.	_____	_____
B. Purim is the most fun Jewish holiday.	_____	_____
C. Soccer is an exciting sport.	_____	_____
D. The most interesting subject in school is math.	_____	_____
E. Jelly doughnuts taste better than latkes.	_____	_____

Show how different opinions can create interesting combinations. In the picture below, fill in the letters that match the opinions with which you *disagree*.

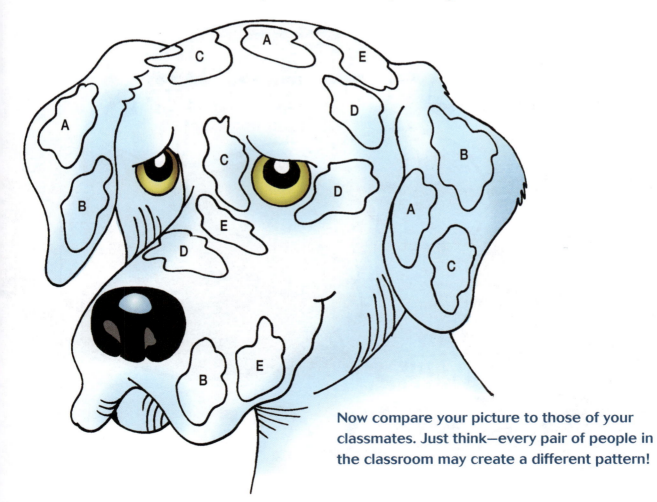

Now compare your picture to those of your classmates. Just think—every pair of people in the classroom may create a different pattern!

CHAPTER 11

Jacob's Discovery

GENESIS 27:42–29:30

אֵלֶּה יַשַׁר בַּמָּקוֹם ...

Genesis 27:42–28:1–10

Rebecca sent for her son Jacob. "Your brother Esau wants to kill you," Rebecca said. "Go to Haran, to the land of my brother Laban. Stay with him until Esau forgets what you have done." Later, Isaac said, "While you are in Haran, find a wife from among Laban's daughters." So Jacob set out for Haran.

GENESIS 28:11–16

As the sun was setting, Jacob stopped for the night. He placed a stone under his head for a pillow. That night he had a dream. In his dream he saw a ladder that stood on the ground and reached up into the heavens. Angels of God were going up and down the ladder. God stood beside Jacob and said, "I am God, the God of Abraham and the God of Isaac. I give this land to you and your descendants. They will spread out to the west and the east, to the north and the south. And remember, I will always be with you and your descendants, and I will protect you wherever you go." Jacob awoke and said, "God is in this place, but I did not know it!"

Think of a place that you consider special. What makes it special? How do you feel when you are there?

In This Place

WORD WIZARD

בַּמָּקוֹם הַזֶּה

A "wake-up call" reminds us of something important. It jolts us, opens our eyes, and shows us something that we had not noticed but was there all along. Jacob's dream was his wake-up call.

In Jacob's dream God reminded him that he was not alone—that God was with him. When he woke up, he realized that God had been *bamakom hazeh*, "in this place," all along. Jacob's dream was a wake-up call to remember that God was not only in this place, but in every place he might be.

GENESIS 29:1–6

Soon Jacob arrived in Haran, the place where his mother had been born. He stopped at a well and spoke to the shepherds there. Jacob asked them, "Do you know Laban the son of Nahor?" "Yes, we do," replied the shepherds. "There is his daughter Rachel now, coming with the flock."

GENESIS 29:10–13

Jacob drew water from the well for Rachel's sheep. He told Rachel that they were cousins. Rachel ran home to tell her father the news. Laban ran to greet his nephew. He hugged and kissed Jacob and took him to his home.

A man and woman meeting at a well? Where have you read that before?

GENESIS 29:15–20

Laban had two daughters. The older one was Leah, and the younger one was Rachel. Jacob fell in love with Rachel. After Jacob had stayed in Haran for a month, Laban said, "You should not watch over my animals for nothing, just because we are family. How should I pay you?" Jacob answered, "I will work for you for seven years. Then allow me to marry your younger daughter Rachel." Laban said, "It is better that she should marry you than a stranger." So Jacob worked for seven years. But because of his love for Rachel, it seemed like only a few days.

How do you think Jacob felt at this moment?

GENESIS 29:21–30

When it came time for the wedding, Laban made a feast. When evening came and Jacob was asleep, Laban brought his daughter Leah to Jacob's tent. When morning came, Jacob saw Leah and not Rachel! "What have you done to me?" Jacob asked Laban. "I was meant to marry Rachel! Why did you trick me?" Laban said, "It is not our custom for the younger daughter to marry before the older. You may marry Rachel as well, if you promise to work another seven years." Jacob promised, and he married Rachel one week later. Though he was married to both sisters, Jacob loved Rachel more than he loved Leah. And he worked for Laban another seven years.

During the bedeken ceremony, the groom lifts the bride's veil from her face. In this way, he avoids making the same mistake as Jacob!

90

This Just In!

TIME TRAVELER

Flashback! **You're a reporter for the** *Haran Gazette*.
You're about to interview three of Haran's most famous citizens:
Rachel, Leah, and Jacob. But first, you'll need questions to ask. For example,
maybe you'll ask Leah how she feels about being part of Laban's trick. Write
one question for each person.

To Rachel: _____

_____

To Leah: _____

_____

To Jacob: _____

Now, switch roles. Answer your questions as you think Rachel, Leah,
and Jacob would have.

_____

Rachel's Answer: _____

Leah's Answer: _____

Jacob's Answer: _____

Trick for Trick

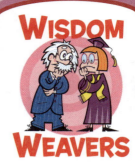

WISDOM WEAVERS

Jacob wanted to marry Rachel but married Leah instead. How could this happen? Let's look for clues in this midrash:

Laban brought his daughter to Jacob's tent and said to Jacob, "Put out the lamp. My daughter is shy." That night, whenever Jacob said, "Rachel," Leah answered. But in the morning, Jacob saw it was Leah. "You tricked me," he said. Leah replied, "You were my teacher. Isaac, your father, called you 'Esau,' and you answered! I learned how to trick from you." (B'reisheet Rabbah 70:19)

When we're dishonest, we pay a price. People lose respect for us. They think twice before believing us again, or before telling us their secrets. Worst of all, we teach others to be dishonest. But dishonesty does not bring peace or justice. Instead, it creates more dishonesty.

When we're honest with one another, we build trust and strengthen friendships.

Honesty Maze

Find the trail to truth and become a trusted friend by completing the Honesty Maze below. Hint: If you come to an honest action, you're going the right way. If you come to a dishonest action, you've reached a dead end and must turn back.

Start

be trustworthy

keep what isn't yours

cheat in a board game

tell the truth

return what isn't yours

blame others for something you did

Become a trusted & respected friend

CHAPTER 12

Jacob's Struggle

GENESIS 31:17–33:10

GENESIS 31:17–18; 32:4–6

Jacob had worked for Laban for twenty years. His years of service were finally over. So he gathered his family, his servants, his animals, and all of his belongings, and he prepared to return to the land of his birth. He sent servants ahead with a message for his brother Esau in the country of Edom. "Tell my brother that I have been living with our uncle Laban in Haran. I send this message in the hope of making peace between us."

Why do you think Jacob wanted to make peace with his brother after all this time?

What do you think will happen to Jacob?

GENESIS 32:7–12

The messengers returned to Jacob. "Esau himself is coming to meet you," they reported, "and there are four hundred men with him." Jacob was very afraid, and he prayed. "God of my father Abraham and God of my father Isaac, rescue me from my brother Esau. I fear that he will come and kill us."

GENESIS 32:14–25

The next day, Jacob sent gifts—including goats, rams, and camels—to his brother Esau. He thought, "If I please Esau with presents, perhaps he will show me kindness." That night, Jacob sent his family across the river Jabbok. And he spent that night in the camp alone.

GENESIS 32:25–30

That night, a stranger wrestled with Jacob. They struggled all night, until the break of dawn. When the stranger saw that he could not defeat Jacob, he twisted Jacob's hip, so that the hip was dislocated. But still Jacob continued to struggle. Then the stranger said, "Let me go—the sun is coming up." But Jacob answered, "I will not let you go unless you bless me!" "What is your name?" asked the stranger. Jacob told the stranger his name. The stranger then said, "Your name will no longer be Jacob, but Israel, for you have struggled with God and with humans, and you have succeeded." And the stranger left that place.

Jacob's New Name
יִשְׂרָאֵל

WORD WIZARD

When big changes happen to people in the Bible, their names sometimes change. Abram became Abraham, meaning *father of nations*. Sarai became Sarah, meaning *princess*. Now, we have what may be the most important change of all: Jacob becomes Israel, meaning *struggles with God*.

When he was born, Jacob grabbed Esau's heel. Then he grabbed his brother's birthright. Then he grabbed his father's blessing. But now he is wiser and more mature. Instead of grabbing what is not his, he now "struggles with God" to understand what God wants and to do what is right.

The Case of the Struggling Stranger

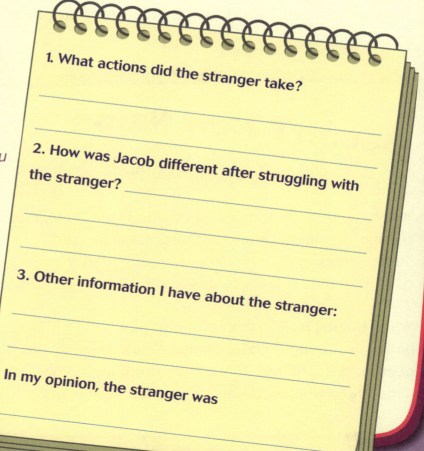

MIDRASH MAKER

Question

The story of Jacob and the stranger is one of the most mysterious in the Torah. Who exactly is the stranger? Why did they struggle?

Classic Midrash

Some rabbis say that the stranger was an angel of God. Because the angels sing to God during the day, the stranger had to leave before dawn. Others say that the stranger was Esau's angel, who came to stop Jacob from reaching his destination. Yet others say that the stranger was God, or perhaps even Jacob himself. (based on various *midrashim*)

Your Midrash

You're a detective. Your job is to gather clues about the Case of the Struggling Stranger. Complete the detective report, including who *you* think the stranger was.

1. What actions did the stranger take? _____

_____

2. How was Jacob different after struggling with the stranger? _____

_____

_____

3. Other information I have about the stranger: _____

_____

In my opinion, the stranger was

_____

GENESIS 33:1–10

The next morning, just after the sunrise, Jacob saw Esau coming toward him with four hundred men. Jacob bowed to the ground seven times as his brother approached. Esau ran toward his brother Jacob and hugged him. They were both so happy that they wept. Esau said, "You did not need to send gifts, my brother. What you have should remain yours." But Jacob said, "No, please accept the gifts. I am so glad to see you. Seeing your face is like seeing the face of God."

In Jacob's time, bowing before someone was a sign of respect. Why do you think Jacob bowed so many times?

The Bible does not explain why Esau greeted his brother so warmly. Perhaps he was impressed by Jacob's gifts. Perhaps he had forgiven his brother. What do you think?

Peace, Brother!

Getting along with a brother or sister can be tough. But by sticking up for your little brother or respecting your big sister's privacy, you can bring peace to your family. Jewish tradition has a name for this special kind of peace: *sh'lom bayit*.

When they were young, Jacob and Esau did not create *sh'lom bayit*. After all, Jacob stole Esau's birthright and their father's blessing, and Esau wanted to kill Jacob. Now, Esau was looking for Jacob—with a small army! But then something amazing happened. Instead of fighting, the brothers made up. It doesn't mean they were no longer angry, or hurt, or upset. It means that they were willing to set aside their differences to achieve what is truly important: *sh'lom bayit*.

The Jewish value of sh'lom bayit *teaches us to seek peace with those who are most important.*

A Full House

We can help to create *sh'lom bayit*—peace in the home—every day. From the list below, select what you consider the four most important ways to create peace in your home. Write one choice in each of the rooms inside the house. Then make up one more of your own and write it in the remaining room.

Keep your room clean

Speak to one another respectfully

Comfort one another in times of sadness

Help with household chores

Celebrate holidays together

Have fun outings as a family

Be a good listener

Respect one another's privacy

CHAPTER 13

The Dreamer

GENESIS 35:16–37:35

עֲלֵי-דַבֵּר לֹו בְּשָׁלֹם
שְׂנֹא אֹתֹו
וַיֹּוסִפוּ עֹוד

GENESIS 35:16–26

Jacob had one daughter, Dinah, and twelve sons: Reuben, Simeon, Levi, Judah, Issachar, Zebulun, Dan, Naphtali, Gad, Asher, Joseph, and Benjamin. After giving birth to Benjamin, Jacob's beloved wife Rachel died.

GENESIS 37:2–4

Jacob loved Joseph the best of his children because he was a comfort to his father in his old age. When Joseph was seventeen, Jacob made him a colorful tunic. When the other brothers saw that Joseph was their father's favorite, they hated him. To make matters worse, Joseph would sometimes bring bad reports of his brothers to their father.

What makes you jealous of a brother, sister, or friend? Why do these things make you jealous?

A Colorful Tunic

כְּתֹנֶת פַּסִּים

WORD WIZARD

Jacob made for Joseph a *k'tonet pasim*—whatever *that* is. No one knows exactly what it was or what it looked like. We know that it was a tunic of some sort, but that's it. Some call it a "coat of many colors." Others call it a "long robe" or "decorated tunic."

The *k'tonet pasim* may be a mystery, but the result is not: By giving Joseph special treatment, Jacob created jealousy among his other sons. That jealousy led to anger and dishonesty. For generations our ancestors have asked: Was Jacob right in giving Joseph the *k'tonet pasim*? What do you think?

Joseph's tunic may have looked like these colorful robes, worn by Egyptian officials.

GENESIS 37:5–8

One day, Joseph told his brothers about a dream he had the night before. "I dreamed that we were in a field," he said. "We were tying bundles of grain. Suddenly, my bundle stood up. Your bundles gathered around and bowed down to mine." His brothers became angry. They asked, "Does that mean that you think you will rule over us?" And they hated Joseph even more.

Why *do you think that* Joseph's brothers felt this way? Did Joseph know that they felt this way? If so, did he care?

GENESIS 37:9–11

Joseph dreamed another dream and told it to his father and brothers. "This time, the sun, moon, and eleven stars were bowing down to me." Now even his father became angry. "What is this dream you have dreamed?" asked his father. "Am I and your brothers supposed to bow to you?" And Joseph's brothers became even more angry.

If you had a dream like this, would you tell your family? Why or why not?

GENESIS 37:12–22

One day, while Joseph's brothers were in the fields tending to the sheep, Jacob said to him, "Go and check on your brothers. Then come back and let me know how they are doing." When Joseph's brothers saw him in the distance, coming toward them, they said to one another, "Here comes the dreamer. Let's kill him and throw him into a pit. We'll say that a wild animal ate him. Then we'll see what becomes of his dreams!" But Reuben, the eldest brother, tried to save Joseph. "We should not kill him," Reuben said. "Throw him into the pit, but do not harm him."

GENESIS 37:23–28

So Joseph's brothers tore off his colorful tunic and threw him into an empty pit. Then they sat down to have a meal. Looking up, they saw a caravan of traders, with camels carrying herbs and spices, on their way to Egypt. Judah said, "What would we gain by killing our brother? Let's sell him to the traders." The brothers agreed. They pulled him out of the pit and sold him to the traders as a slave. The traders took Joseph to Egypt.

GENESIS 37:31–35

Then the brothers dipped Joseph's colorful tunic in goat's blood and took the tunic to their father. "We found this," they said to their father. "Please look at it. Is this Joseph's tunic?" Jacob recognized

Trickery seems to follow Jacob everywhere! Think of a time he tricked others, and a time he himself was tricked.

Who Am I?

Flashback! **You're back in the time of Joseph. Match each quote to the person who might have said it.**

Jacob

Reuben

Judah

Joseph

I don't understand why my brothers hate me. It's not my fault that I'm better than they are!

I tricked others, and then I was tricked myself. Even my sons tricked me!

I don't have a problem getting rid of our brother, but why not get paid for it?

My brothers have gone too far. I'm the eldest son, and I should set an example.

it—it was the very one he had made for Joseph. "Joseph's tunic! A wild animal has eaten him! My son has been torn to shreds!" Jacob was so upset that even his children could not comfort him. "I will mourn for Joseph for the rest of my life," said Jacob.

The Humble Mountain

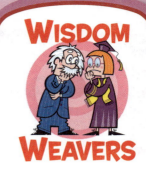

One midrash tells this story: When God was choosing a mountain on which to deliver the Torah, all the mountains began to boast. "I am the tallest," said one mountain. "I am the steepest," said another. Each of the mountains found a reason why it should be chosen. But God chose Mount Sinai—not because it was the tallest or the grandest mountain, but because it was the most humble.

When Joseph was young, he was not like the humble Mount Sinai. Instead, he was boastful. He was not concerned with the feelings of his father and brothers. He was concerned only with himself.

When we forget to be humble, we can forget to share.

108

Say It Again!

Joseph was not only confident in himself, he was also boastful. His confidence would help him to become a strong person. But his boasting only made others angry.

The two people below are boasting. Help them to express themselves in a confident but humble way. We've done the first one for you.

I love my personality—don't you?

I love to make people laugh.

I am the greatest tennis player in the world!

we're great at tennis
are

Of course I'll pass the spelling test—I'm a genius!

I'll try my best

The teacher likes me more than anyone else in the class!

I'm a good kid

CHAPTER 14

Joseph's Gift

GENESIS 39:1–41:57

מקץ

פרשת

GENESIS 39:1–6

Once the traders arrived in Egypt, they sold Joseph as a slave. He now belonged to an Egyptian named Potiphar, who was an officer of Pharaoh, the king of Egypt. God was with Joseph. Joseph became successful at everything he did. Potiphar was so impressed that he made Joseph his head servant.

What do you think it means that "God was with Joseph"? Have you ever felt that God was with you? When?

111

First, Joseph was thrown into a pit. Now he is thrown in jail. What do the two events have in common?

GENESIS 39:6–20

Joseph was very handsome, and Potiphar's wife liked to look at him. One day, when they were alone, she said to Joseph, "Kiss me." Joseph said no. "Your husband, my master, has placed his trust in me. I cannot betray his trust, and I cannot commit this sin before God." Potiphar's wife grew angry. She lied to Potiphar, saying that Joseph had tried to kiss *her*. Potiphar threw Joseph into Pharaoh's jail.

GENESIS 40:1–8

In jail, time passed slowly for Joseph. One day, he noticed that a fellow prisoner—Pharaoh's former butler—looked upset. "What is wrong?" Joseph asked him. "I had a dream," the butler told Joseph, "and there is no one to explain what it means." Joseph said, "God can! Please, tell me your dream."

GENESIS 40:9–23

"In my dream," the butler said, "there was a vine with three branches. Suddenly, clusters of grapes appeared on the vine. I squeezed the grapes into a wine cup, and I gave the cup to Pharaoh." Joseph said, "This is what your dream means: In three days, Pharaoh will take you out of jail, and you will once again be his butler. But please, when you are free, tell Pharaoh about me. Tell him that I have done nothing wrong." What Joseph said came true, and the butler was freed from jail. But the butler forgot all about Joseph.

GENESIS 41:1–7

Two years passed. One night, Pharaoh had two dreams. In the first, he saw seven fat, healthy cows come up from the Nile. They grazed on the green grass by the river. Then suddenly, seven ugly, skinny cows came up from the water and swallowed up the seven fat cows. In Pharaoh's second dream, seven healthy ears of corn grew on one stalk. But then seven skinny and sickly ears of corn came up and swallowed up the seven healthy ears.

GENESIS 41:8–13

Pharaoh sent for all the magicians and wise men of Egypt to explain the meaning of his dreams, but no one could. Then the butler spoke up. "Pardon me for not saying this before," he said. "In prison, there was a young Hebrew slave. I told him my dream, and he told me the meaning. And what he said came true!"

The Pharaohs of ancient Egypt were considered to be children of Ra, the Egyptian sun god.

Genesis 41:14–32

So Pharaoh sent for Joseph. "I have heard that you can hear a dream and tell its meaning," said Pharaoh. Joseph answered, "Not me! But God can help you." Then Pharaoh told Joseph his two dreams. Joseph said, "Both of Pharaoh's dreams have the same meaning. The seven healthy cows and the seven healthy ears of corn are seven years of rich harvests. After that, very little food will grow. The hunger will be so terrible that no one will remember the years of plenty. God is telling Pharaoh what will happen."

Genesis 41:33–49

"This is what Pharaoh should do," Joseph continued. "Find a wise man to prepare for the years of hunger. Save up food from the years of rich harvests, so that Egypt will survive the years of hunger that will follow." Pharaoh said to Joseph, "There is no one as wise as you. I will appoint you as that leader. You will be my second in command. Everyone in all of Egypt will obey you." During the seven years of plenty, Joseph stored up the grain—so much that it could not be measured.

Genesis 41:53–57

Then the seven years of plenty came to an end. Just as Joseph had predicted, seven years of hunger set in. Joseph opened the storehouses of grain and rationed it out to the Egyptians.

Meanwhile, the years of hunger spread out to other places in the world. Everyone, including Joseph's own family, came to Joseph in Egypt to buy food.

Joseph's Life Story

Flashback! **You are an Egyptian historian, living at the time of Joseph. Tell the story of Joseph's life by numbering the following pictures from 1 through 5.**

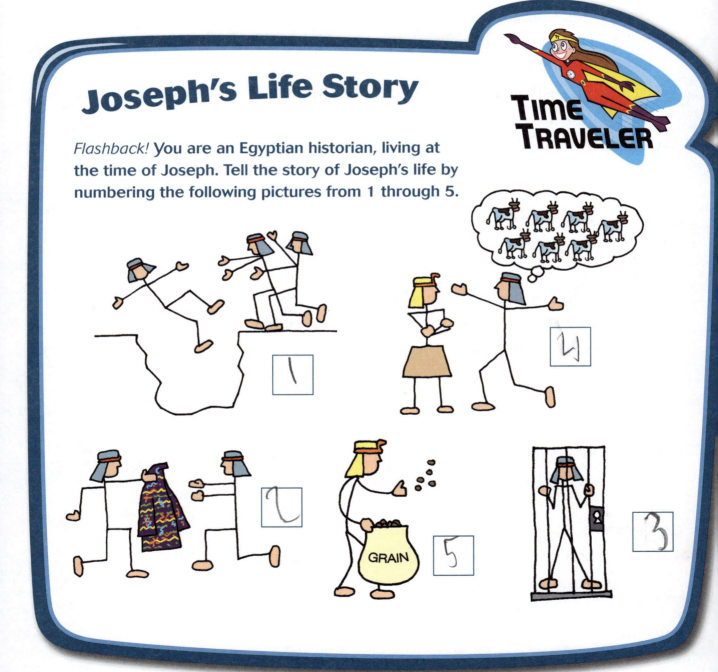

Joseph's New Job

Question

Why did Pharaoh appoint Joseph to be his second in command?
Joseph was only a slave!

Classic Midrash

Pharaoh's wise men gave him only bad news. One predicted that Pharaoh would
have seven daughters who would marry seven brothers, all of whom would fight
Pharaoh for power. One said that Pharaoh would have seven children, one of
whom was going to kill him. The wise men argued with one another over who
was right and who was wrong—and no one offered a plan to prevent disaster.

But Joseph was different. Joseph gave bad news, but he also offered a plan
to deal with it. And he gave credit to God, not himself. Joseph's wisdom and
modesty impressed Pharaoh, and that was why he made him second in
command over all of Egypt. (B'reisheet Rabbah 89:7)

Your Midrash

Imagine this: Even before he met Joseph, Pharaoh had been looking for a
leader to stand by his side. Help Pharaoh find the perfect person by writing
as many words as you can that describe a good leader:

smart

patient

wise   nice   trying

going forit   hardworking.

Now, circle three of your words that also describe Joseph.

The Greatest Gift of All

Think of an interesting dream of your own. What did it mean? Did it answer a question? Tell the future? If you lived at the time of Joseph, you might have brought these questions to a *dream interpreter*. Many people believed that dream interpreters had a special gift that other people did not. Joseph was Egypt's greatest dream interpreter. It was his special gift.

Like Joseph, you have special gifts. Perhaps you can dance or write stories or cheer people up when they feel sad. Or help fix a computer problem. Or teach the *alef-bet*. You might even have gifts that you don't yet know about. And just as Joseph shared his gift with all of Egypt, so too can you share your gift with *your* community—and make it stronger than ever.

Maybe you have a gift for bringing smiles to people's faces.

118

Share Your Gifts

We each have gifts—talents and abilities—that we can share with others. If you enjoy art, how can you use your talent to cheer up a friend? If you're a great soccer player, how could you use your ability to help a teammate? On each box, draw or write about a gift you could share. On each tag, write the name of the person receiving your "gift."

CHAPTER 15

Joseph's Forgiveness

GENESIS 41:53–46:7

GENESIS 41:53–42:5

Joseph's predictions came true. Egypt enjoyed seven years of good harvests and then suffered seven years of famine. Because Joseph had planned wisely, however, the Egyptians had plenty of food. But those in the land of Canaan, where Jacob and his family lived, had not prepared. Everyone was hungry. "Don't just stand around looking at one another," Jacob said to his sons one day. "Go down to Egypt and buy food, so that we may have enough to live." So ten of Joseph's eleven brothers went down to Egypt. Jacob was afraid that something terrible might happen to Benjamin, his youngest son, and so he kept him at home.

Genesis 42:6–8

When the brothers arrived in Egypt, they went to the officer in charge of distributing food. They bowed before him. Because many years had passed, they did not recognize Joseph. But Joseph recognized *them*. He pretended not to know them, however, and he spoke to them in harsh tones. "Where do you come from?" he asked. "From the land of Canaan," his brothers replied, "to buy food."

Genesis 42:9–24

Joseph said, "You are spies!" "No, my lord," said the brothers. "Truly, we have come to buy food. We are honest men, sons of a man who lives in the land of Canaan. Our youngest brother is with our father, and one brother is no more." But Joseph said, "I still believe that you are spies. So I will test you. One of you will remain here. The rest of you will return to Canaan with food for your starving households. If you return to me with your youngest brother, you may all go free." And Joseph ordered his servants to take his brother Simeon as a prisoner.

Why did Joseph choose Simeon? According to one midrash, it was Simeon who had thrown Joseph into the pit.

GENESIS 42:29–43:1

Jacob's sons returned home and explained to their father what had happened. "Joseph is gone and Simeon is gone," Jacob said. "And now you want to take away Benjamin! Why do these things always happen to me? No, Benjamin will not go with you to Egypt. If something were to happen to him, I would die of grief!" But the hunger in the land of Canaan grew worse.

GENESIS 43:2–14

When all the food from Egypt was gone, Jacob said to his sons, "Go back and buy more food." But Judah reminded him, "We can only buy more food if you let Benjamin go with us. Please, I will be responsible for him." "Very well," Jacob said. "Take gifts for the man—the best fruit of the land, as well as honey, pistachios, and almonds. And may God see to it that the man shows mercy and allows both Simeon and Benjamin to return home."

Jacob sent gifts of honey, almonds, and pistachios to Egypt, even though his family was hungry. Why do you think he did this?

Remember Joseph's dream of the eleven stars bowing down to him? In a way, the dream has come true.

GENESIS 43:15–33

Once again, the brothers came before Joseph. Again, they bowed before him. "Prepare a meal," Joseph said to his servant, "for they will dine with me today." Before the meal, Joseph's brothers gave him their gifts. Joseph brought Simeon to them. Joseph told the brothers where to sit, from the eldest to the youngest. The men were amazed. How did the man know their ages?

Genesis 44:1–13

After the meal, Joseph tested his brothers once again. He said to his servant, "Fill the men's bags with food for their journey home. And place my silver goblet in the bag of Benjamin, the youngest." Then, as his brothers left the city, Joseph ordered his servant to arrest them and bring them back. Again the servant did as Joseph said.

Genesis 44:14–45:4

Joseph said to his brothers, "One of you has stolen my silver goblet. How could you do such a thing? Whoever has the goblet will become my slave. The others may go free." Joseph's servant searched their bags, one by one. They found the goblet in Benjamin's bag. When the brothers saw this, they were terrified. Judah said, "Please, my lord, our father is very old. He has already lost one son. If we return without Benjamin, his youngest, he will die of grief. Please, take me as a slave instead, but allow the boy to return home." At that point, Joseph could no longer control himself. He sent his servants from the room, and he began to cry. He said to his brothers, "I am your brother Joseph, whom you sold into slavery." His brothers were so surprised that they could not answer.

How would you have felt if you were one of Joseph's brothers? Would you have been afraid that he would still be angry? Would you have been happy to see that he was alive?

GENESIS 45:5–15

"Do not blame yourselves for selling me into slavery," Joseph explained to his brothers. "God sent me here to save many people from hunger. So it was not you who sent me here, but God. Please, hurry back to my father and tell him everything that you have seen, and bring him here quickly. Tell him that his son Joseph says: 'You will live here, in Egypt. You will be near me—you, your family, and everything that you have. I will take care of you.'" Then Joseph embraced his brothers, and they all wept.

GENESIS 45:25–28

Joseph's brothers returned home and told their father, "Joseph is still alive. In fact, he rules over the land of Egypt!" At first, Jacob did not believe them. But when he saw the wagons that Joseph had sent for them, his spirits rose. "My son Joseph is still alive!" he said. "I will see him before I die."

GENESIS 46:5–7

This is how Jacob's family came to settle in the land of Egypt. They had many children and increased in the land, just as God had promised.

Family Reunion

Flashback! You are witnessing the reunion between Joseph and his father, Jacob. You know that they have not seen each other in many years. Fill in the bubbles with what you think they might say.

The first words Joseph and Jacob say to each other:

One question you'd like to ask either Jacob or Joseph:

Forgive Me!

It can be hard to get along with friends and siblings. We hurt one another's feelings, damage our relationships, and sometimes make a giant mess. Sometimes we're so angry and upset that it seems as if we'll go on fighting forever. It can be even harder to forgive. It takes courage to rise above our anger and our hurt feelings.

Joseph's brothers sold him into slavery. *That* was hard to forgive. But Joseph rose above his anger and his hurt to forgive his brothers. *That* took courage.

On Yom Kippur, the Day of Atonement, some people gently beat their chests as they recite the Al Ḥet, a prayer asking God for forgiveness.

Forgiveness Chat

Jamie and Dana got into an argument today at school. They both want to apologize, but it's hard. Help them find the right words by entering the chat room below and filling in the blanks.

QuickSketch: I'm upset about what happened today at school. You too?

FotoFan: Yes. I got really mad when you said what you said. It made me feel _____.

QuickSketch: I know. That's why I want to say _____

_____.

FotoFan: I feel the same way. How can we make sure this doesn't happen again?

QuickSketch: I'll make sure not to _____

_____.

FotoFan: Good plan. See ya!

CHAPTER 16

Baby Moses

EXODUS 1:1–2:10

וַתֹּאמֶרְלָה בַּת־פַּרְעֹה לְכִי

EXODUS 1:1–11

Joseph and his brothers had many children, and *their* children had many children. The Israelites became numerous in the land of Egypt. Time passed, and a new Pharaoh now ruled the land. He did not know about Joseph or what he had done for Egypt. "There are too many Israelites," he said. "If there is a war, they may rise up against us." So Pharaoh made the Israelites slaves.

The children of Jacob were known as Israelites. Sometimes they were called Hebrews. Many years later, they would be called Jews.

EXODUS 1:11–22

All day long the Israelites built cities for Pharaoh. The Egyptians made life bitter and hard for the Israelites, but still the Israelite community grew. One day Pharaoh spoke to two midwives, women who helped deliver babies. "If the baby is a girl," Pharaoh told them, "she may live. But if the baby is a boy, kill him." But the midwives did not obey Pharaoh. Instead, they let the boys live. So Pharaoh gave an order to all his people. "If a Hebrew woman gives birth to a boy," he said, "throw him into the Nile River."

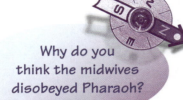

Why do you think the midwives disobeyed Pharaoh?

EXODUS 2:1–4

During this terrible time, a woman named Yocheved and a man named Amram had a son. Yocheved hid the baby, afraid that he would be taken from her and killed. After three months, she could hide him no longer. She took a wicker basket, sealed it with tar to make it float, put the boy inside, and placed it in the Nile. Her daughter Miriam, the baby's sister, stood at a distance to see what would happen.

Bouncing Back

MIDRASH MAKER

Question
How did the Israelites manage to flourish, even though the Egyptians "made life bitter" for them?

Classic Midrash
The Egyptians not only wanted the Israelites to work hard, they also wanted to break their spirit. They made children carry the loads of grown men. They forced old women to carry the loads of young women. The only rewards the Israelites received for their work were kicks and curses.

But the Israelites remained proud of who they were. They did not change their names or their language, and they did not turn on one another. In this way, the Israelites flourished—and became a strong community. (Sh'mot Rabbah 1:15)

Your Midrash
Sometimes when we are faced with a challenge, we try even harder to succeed. Imagine that you are an Israelite slave. List three ways that the cruel treatment by the Egyptians can make your community stronger.

1. _____

_____

2. _____

_____

3. _____

_____

Ark & Basket

תֵּבָה

WORD WIZARD

The word *tevah* means both "ark" and "basket." It first appears in the Torah when Noah builds his ark. Now it appears again, when Moses floats down the Nile in his basket. Could it be that these two stories have something in common?

Moses, like Noah, lived in a time of great danger. Moses, like Noah, floated in a *tevah* that carried him to dry land, to safety. And Moses, like Noah, would begin a new and important period in our history.

EXODUS 2:5–10

After a while, Pharaoh's daughter came down to bathe in the Nile. She saw the basket and sent a servant to bring it out. When she opened it, she saw that it was a child—a baby boy. "This must be a Hebrew child!" she exclaimed. Then Miriam stepped forward. She said to Pharaoh's daughter, "Would you like me to find a Hebrew nurse to help you care for the child?" "Yes," said Pharaoh's daughter. So Miriam went and returned with her mother. Pharaoh's daughter named the baby Moses, explaining, "I drew him out of the water."

The words "I drew" give us a hint of what Moses will do later, when he will "draw" the Israelites from Egypt.

The Nile River has always been
very important to Egypt. It provides
water for crops, for drinking, and
for making bricks to build homes.

Sticking Together

What would have become of Moses if the Egyptian midwives hadn't saved Israelite babies? Or if Yocheved hadn't hidden the baby Moses? Or if Miriam hadn't seen him to safety? Or if Pharaoh's daughter hadn't rescued him from the Nile? Moses survived because each woman did her part and did the right thing.

Our sages teach, "You are not required to finish the task, nor are you allowed to stop trying." Like these brave women, each of us must do our part to see that people are treated fairly and that justice is done.

When we work together as a team, we can reach new heights.

136

Planting a Seed

Your class is having a party on Tu B'shevat, the Jewish celebration of trees and the environment. During the party, the class will take a short hike outside, plant a tree, and eat fruits that are grown in Israel.

In the list below, circle the names of students who are doing their part to create a great party. Then fill in their spaces inside the circle. What do you see?

A. Terry brings in a sapling to plant in the ground.
B. Marty drops a candy wrapper on the ground during the hike.
C. Ashley talks while the teacher explains the meaning of Tu B'shevat.
D. David brings in a watering can and a shovel.
E. Gila calls everyone in the class to remind them about the party.
F. Ralph forgets about the party and goes to the movies instead.
G. Vicki creates a schedule to make sure the sapling is watered every week.
H. Jeremy brings in dates, figs, and grapes for the class to enjoy.
I. Don eats all the grapes.

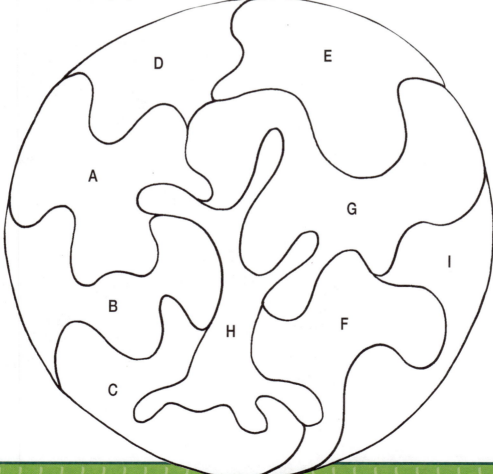

CHAPTER 17

Moses Stands Before God

Exodus 2:11–4:18

מעשה
משה

EXODUS 2:11–12

Years passed. Moses grew up in Pharaoh's palace as a prince of Egypt. One day, he saw an Egyptian beating a Hebrew slave. Moses felt pity for the slave, who was one of his people. Moses looked around. Seeing that no one was watching, he killed the Egyptian and hid his body in the sand.

In your opinion, did Moses do the right thing? Why?

139

One of His People

מֵאֶחָיו

Moses had likely never seen the Israelite slave before. But the Torah calls the man *mei'eḥav*, "one of his people." Why? Did Moses know that he himself was an Israelite? Did Pharaoh's daughter tell him? Did his parents tell him? Did he somehow figure it out? We don't know.

What we do know is that Moses felt a responsibility to help the slave. He knew it was wrong to treat others so harshly. The Egyptians who held the whips may have been Moses's neighbors, but those who deserved justice were truly "his people."

EXODUS 2:13–15

The next day, Moses saw two Hebrew slaves fighting with each other. He said to one, "Why do you strike your neighbor?" The slave replied, "Who made you ruler over us? Are you going to kill me like you killed the Egyptian?" Moses became frightened. He realized that others knew what he had done. Before long, Pharaoh found out. He wanted to kill Moses, so Moses ran away.

EXODUS 2:15–25

Moses settled in the land of Midian. He married Zipporah, the daughter of Jethro the Priest, and together they had children. Moses stayed in Midian for many years. Meanwhile, in Egypt, the Pharaoh who knew Moses had died, and the new Pharaoh treated the Israelites even more harshly. The Israelites cried out, and their cry for help rose up to God. God heard their groaning and remembered the covenant made with Abraham and Isaac and Jacob.

Reminder: God's covenant with Abraham was, "I will make of you a great nation… This land will belong to your descendants forever."

EXODUS 3:1–6

One day, while taking care of Jethro's sheep, Moses came to Mount Horeb, also called Mount Sinai. While there, he saw a strange sight: a bush that was on fire but did not burn up. "I must look at this strange sight," Moses said. "Why doesn't the bush burn up?" Then God called to him from the bush: "Moses! Moses!" Moses answered, "Here I am." And God said, "Do not come closer. Remove your sandals from your feet, for the place on which you are standing is holy ground. I am the God of your father, the God of Abraham, the God of Isaac, and the God of Jacob." Moses hid his face. He was afraid to look at God.

Like Abraham when *he* was called upon by God, Moses says *hineni*, "here I am." He is showing God that he is giving his full attention and is ready to listen.

EXODUS 3:7–12

God continued, "I have seen the suffering of My people in Egypt. I will take them out of Egypt, to a land flowing with milk and honey. I will send you to Pharaoh, and you will free My people, the Israelites, from Egypt." But Moses said, "Who am I that I should go to Pharaoh and free the Israelites?" God said, "I will be with you."

EXODUS 4:1–5

Moses said, "But what if the Israelites do not believe that You really sent me?" God said, "Take the staff in your hand and throw it to the ground." Moses threw the staff to the ground, and it became a snake. Moses jumped back. Then God said, "Put out your hand and grasp it by the tail." Moses did so, and the snake became a staff in his hand. "This is how they will know that I have sent you," said God.

Dangerous snakes are usually picked up by their necks. Why do you think God asked Moses to grab the snake by its tail?

This 2,000-year-old wall painting shows slaves laboring in Egypt. How do you think it felt to be a slave?

143

EXODUS 4:10–17

Then Moses said to God, "But I do not speak well. I am slow of speech and slow of tongue. And also, how will I know what to say?" God said, "I will be with you, and I will tell you what to say." But Moses said, "Please, God, choose someone else." God became angry with Moses. "Your brother Aaron will speak for you," God said. "Right now he is coming to meet you, and he will be happy to see you. Now, take this staff, with which you will perform the miracles."

EXODUS 4:18

Moses went to his father-in-law Jethro and said, "Let me return to my people in Egypt." And Jethro said to Moses, "Go in peace."

Think about a time when you, like Moses, tried to avoid responsibility. Why did you do so?

Why Me?

Question

Why did Moses ask God to choose someone else?

Classic Midrash

When he was a child, Moses grabbed Pharaoh's crown and placed it upon his own head. Pharaoh was worried. Perhaps this was a sign that Moses would one day replace him. So Pharaoh arranged a test for Moses. A bright jewel and a hot coal were placed before the child. If Moses chose the jewel, it was a sign that he would be a threat—and must be put to death.

Moses reached for the jewel. But an angel pushed his hand toward the coal. Moses chose the hot coal and was spared. But the hot coal burned his hand. To cool it off, Moses stuck his hand, along with the burning coal, in his mouth. Thus, his lips and tongue were burned and his speech was affected. Because of this, he asked God to choose someone else. (Sh'mot Rabbah 1:26)

Your Midrash

Sometimes, when we're afraid to do something, we think of reasons to avoid the task. Maybe that's why Moses made the excuses he did. Help Moses to feel less afraid by giving him three reasons why he is the right person for the job.

1. _____
_____

2. _____
_____

3. _____
_____

Rise Up!

Next year, or the year after that, or maybe the year after that, you will begin your bar or bat mitzvah training. You will learn to read portions of the Bible in Hebrew. You will learn to lead the congregation in prayer. You will become, for what may be the first time, a leader in your community.

Like Moses, you may be afraid. Like Moses, you may hesitate. Like Moses, you may even create excuses: It's too hard! I can't speak well! But just as Moses will rise to his challenge, so will you. And just as Moses did, you will make the community stronger.

During your bar or bat mitzvah ceremony, you will rise to the bimah, *rise to the Torah, and rise to the challenge before you.*

146

It's No Excuse

The kids below are thinking of excuses that people use all the time to avoid tough challenges. You've decided: No more excuses! Help them to think about their challenges in a different way.

I can't speak in front of everyone! It's too scary.

There's too much homework to do. I'll never finish! I think I'll watch TV.

I'll never be good enough to play in the concert. Why even try?

CHAPTER 18

Freedom and the Future

EXODUS 5:1–12:42

וּפָסַח

יְיָ עַל

הַפֶּתַח

EXODUS 5:1–6:1

Moses and his brother Aaron stood before Pharaoh. They said to him, "The God of Israel says, 'Let My people go.'" Pharaoh grew angry, saying, "Why should I listen to God? I do not know God, and I will not let the Israelites go." Then he told the taskmasters, "You may no longer give the slaves straw to make bricks. But they must make the same number as before." Then God said to Moses, "I will force Pharaoh to let My people go. He will even *want* to drive them out."

Think of five things you like to do. Which of those things could you do if you were a slave?

149

EXODUS 7:10–13

Again, Moses and Aaron came before Pharaoh. Aaron threw down his staff, and it became a serpent. Pharaoh summoned the magicians of Egypt. They also threw down their staffs, and they also became serpents. Pharaoh's heart hardened, and he would not let the Israelites go.

EXODUS 7:19–22

Then God told Moses, "Say to Aaron: Lift your staff over the waters of Egypt—its rivers, its canals, and its ponds." Moses and Aaron did as God commanded. As Pharaoh watched, the Nile River turned to blood. But Pharaoh's magicians also turned water to blood. Again Pharaoh's heart hardened, and he would not let the people go. Turning the Nile to blood was God's first plague on Egypt.

EXODUS 8:1–2

Then God told Moses, "Say to Aaron: Lift your staff over the rivers and the ponds, and bring up frogs to the land of Egypt." Moses and Aaron did as God commanded, and frogs came up and covered the land. Covering the land with frogs was God's second plague on Egypt.

Imagine what it must have been like to be surrounded by frogs!

150

EXODUS 8:4–11

Then Pharaoh said to Moses, "Tell your God to remove the frogs, and I will let the people go." Moses cried out to God to stop the frogs. All over Egypt, the frogs died. But again Pharaoh's heart hardened, and he would not let the people go.

EXODUS 8:12–9:12

God brought more plagues on the land of Egypt. The third plague turned dust to lice, which crawled over people and animals. The fourth plague sent swarms of insects to invade the country. The fifth plague struck cattle with disease, so that all the livestock of Egypt died. The sixth plague caused boils to break out on people's skin. All over Egypt people cried out in pain. But after each new plague, Pharaoh's heart hardened, and he would not let the Israelites go.

The Torah tells us that the plagues struck the Egyptians only. The Israelites remained safe.

EXODUS 9:18–35

God's seventh plague on Egypt was hail. The hail was so heavy that fire flashed down with it, and the trees of the field burned. Finally, Pharaoh said to Moses and Aaron, "God is right, and I am wrong! Please ask God to stop the hail. Then I will let you go." Moses did this. But when Pharaoh saw that the hail had stopped, his heart hardened. Again, he would not let the Israelites go.

Exodus 10:4–20

"If you still refuse," Moses and Aaron said to Pharaoh, "God will bring locusts. There will be so many that no one will be able to see the land." This time, Pharaoh's servants spoke up. "Please, let their people go. Our land is being destroyed!" But Pharaoh refused. When morning came, a cloud of locusts ate all the grass and all the fruit in Egypt. But again Pharaoh's heart hardened, and he would not let the Israelites go.

Exodus 10:21–27

Then God said to Moses, "Lift your arm toward the sky. There will be darkness over Egypt, a darkness so thick that you can *feel* it." For three days, it was so dark that people hardly moved. But there was light in the homes of the Israelites. Then Pharaoh said to Moses, "Go! Be gone! But leave your animals here." Moses said, "No, not a single animal will remain behind." Again Pharaoh's heart was hardened, and he would not let the Israelites go.

Why *do* you think that Moses refused to leave without the animals?

Even today, swarms of locusts sometimes attack Egypt and nearby countries. A swarm can contain as many as one hundred million locusts and eat as many as one hundred million pounds of crops in a single night. No wonder Pharaoh's servants begged him to let the Israelites go.

Exodus 11:1–6

God said to Moses, "I will bring one more plague upon Egypt. After that, Pharaoh will let you go. In fact, he will chase you out. Toward midnight, every firstborn Egyptian will die, including the firstborn of Pharaoh. There will be a loud cry in the land of Egypt, a cry that has never been heard and will never be heard again."

Exodus 12:1–27

God said to Moses and Aaron, "Tonight I will go through Egypt and strike down every firstborn son in Egypt. Speak to the community of Israel. Tell them that each family should take the blood of a lamb and put it on the doorposts of their houses. When I see the blood, I will pass over them. This day will be a day of remembrance. You will celebrate it as a festival to God forever, for on this day I brought you out of Egypt."

What is the name of that festival? Why is this festival important?

EXODUS 12:30–34

That night, Pharaoh woke to a loud cry. In almost every house, someone had died. Finally, Pharaoh said to Moses and Aaron, "Go! Leave, you and all the Israelites with you!" The Egyptians hurried the Israelites to leave, afraid that more terrible things would happen if they stayed. The Israelites gathered together and they left Egypt. They left so quickly that the people took their dough from their ovens before it could rise.

EXODUS 12:40–42

The Israelites had been slaves in Egypt for four hundred and thirty years when they left Egypt. That night was a holy night for God and for the children of Israel for all time.

When we eat matzah, we imagine that we too were slaves fleeing Egypt.

We Should Never Forget

Flashback! You are an Israelite, preparing to leave Egypt. You have an idea: You will write a letter to kids who live thousands of years from now. Explain how you feel to be free for the first time. How do you think life will be better? How will it be harder?

Looking Ahead

WISDOM WEAVERS

We have reached a special moment in the Bible. For the first time, God speaks of the Israelites as *adat yisrael*—the **community** of Israel. As a community, the Israelites have suffered together. As a community, they have celebrated the first Passover. Now, as a community, they will be free.

The Israelites now face an important challenge. They are no longer slaves, and there is much to look forward to. But being a community requires looking together toward the future. A community is strongest when it shares its dreams—and works together to make those dreams come true.

What will happen to Moses and the Israelites as they look to their future? We'll find out.

A community is strongest when it looks together toward the future.

To the Future!

Complete the sentences to learn how we can build a strong future.
Then find the new words inside the word search. Words may appear
in any direction—including diagonally and upside-down!

1. Show support for __I__ ___ ___ ___ ___ ___, the Jewish homeland.

2. Remember God's promise to Abraham that Jews will
   "be like the specks of dust on the __E__ ___ ___ ___ ___—too many to count."

3. Study the __T__ ___ ___ ___ ___ with your family and classmates.

4. Light Shabbat __C__ ___ ___ ___ ___ ___ ___ together.

5. Learn __H__ ___ ___ ___ ___ ___, the language of the Bible.

6. Create __S__ ___ ___ ___ ___ ___, which means "peace."

7. Come together in the synagogue to __P__ ___ ___ ___ together.

8. During the __P__ ___ ___ ___ ___ ___ ___ ___ seder, remember that
   we were once slaves, but now we are free.

9. Remember that each of us is an important member of the
   Jewish __C__ ___ ___ ___ ___ ___ ___ ___ __y__.

```
K P C Q B T Y E C Z K A
Z E A R T H T E A S O Y
R M Y S B A R V N W N I
W A H S S J A R D L W K
E F E H K O C O L T P H
R W L A V J V O E S N P
B P T L Y N U E S X R G
E P B O H P I S R A E L
H R G M R S C Z Y P O D
J A T A K A K O A U J Q
R E Y R S I H O T A J R
C O M M U N I T Y S E U
```

157

Who's Who

Adam   Eve

Adam and **Eve** were the first man and woman. They disobeyed God by eating from the Tree of Knowledge of Good and Evil. They were cast out of the Garden of Eden.

Cain and **Abel** were sons of Adam and Eve. God accepted Abel's sacrifice but not Cain's. Cain killed his brother.

Cain   Abel

Noah

God planned to send a flood to destroy the earth. God chose a righteous man, **Noah**, to build an ark that would carry his family and two of every animal to safety.

Abraham

God promised **Abraham** and **Sarah** that they would be the father and mother of nations. The Jewish people would come forth from them.

Sarah

Isaac

Isaac was the son of Abraham and Sarah. He married **Rebecca**, a woman of great kindness.

Rebecca

Jacob

Jacob and **Esau** were the sons of Isaac and Rebecca. Jacob tricked his father into blessing him instead of his brother Esau. Jacob married Leah and Rachel.

Esau

Joseph

Joseph was the son of Jacob and Rachel. Joseph's brothers sold him into slavery. He interpreted Pharaoh's dreams, became a leader of Egypt, and saved his family from famine.

Moses, the son of Israelite slaves, was raised by the daughter of Pharaoh. God chose Moses to lead the Israelites out of Egypt.

Moses

DESMOND COLE
GHOST PATROL

THE SLEEPWALKING SNOWMAN

by Andres Miedoso

illustrated by Victor Rivas

LITTLE SIMON

New York London Toronto Sydney New Delhi

LITTLE SIMON

An imprint of Simon & Schuster Children's Publishing Division
1230 Avenue of the Americas, New York, New York 10020
First Little Simon paperback edition March 2019
Copyright © 2019 by Simon & Schuster, Inc.
Also available in a Little Simon hardcover edition.
All rights reserved, including the right of reproduction in whole or in part in any form.
LITTLE SIMON is a registered trademark of Simon & Schuster, Inc.,
and associated colophon is a trademark of Simon & Schuster, Inc.
For information about special discounts for bulk purchases, please contact
Simon & Schuster Special Sales at 1-866-506-1949 or business@simonandschuster.com.
The Simon & Schuster Speakers Bureau can bring authors to your live event. For more information
or to book an event contact the Simon & Schuster Speakers Bureau at 1-866-248-3049 or
visit our website at www.simonspeakers.com.
Designed by Steve Scott
Manufactured in the United States of America 0219 MTN
2 4 6 8 10 9 7 5 3 1
Library of Congress Cataloging-in-Publication Data
Names: Miedoso, Andres, author. | Rivas, Victor, illustrator.
Title: The sleepwalking snowman / by Andres Miedoso ; illustrated by Victor Rivas.
Description: First Little Simon hardcover edition. | New York : Little Simon, [2019] |
Series: Desmond Cole ghost patrol ; 7 | Summary: Desmond and Andres face a snowman
that was built by a schoolmate but seems to have a mind of its own,
as well as a snowball-throwing bully.
Identifiers: LCCN 2018036952 | ISBN 9781534433472 (paperback) |
ISBN 9781534433489 (hc) | ISBN 9781534433496 (eBook)
Subjects: | CYAC: Snowmen—Fiction. | Winter—Fiction. | Bullying—Fiction. |
Friendship—Fiction. | African Americans—Fiction. |
Hispanic Americans—Fiction. | BISAC: JUVENILE FICTION / Action & Adventure / General. |
JUVENILE FICTION / Readers / Chapter Books.
Classification: LCC PZ7.1.M518 Sle 2019 | DDC [Fic]—dc23
LC record available at https://lccn.loc.gov/2018036952

CONTENTS

CHAPTER ONE

WINTER IS WEIRD

Winter is weird, isn't it?

At first, everything is great! There's a chill in the air. The first snowfall covers the world like a white, fluffy blanket. Even the smell of winter is awesome.

And there are so many things to do:

like snowball fights, skiing, playing hockey, sledding, skating, and even making snowmen.

Then at night there is nothing better than warming up in front of a roaring fireplace.

Winter is *the best*!

At least it's the best until the snow gets all dirty and gross. Then the streets get icy and slippery, and it gets so windy outside, you can't even keep your eyes open.

The days get shorter. It gets dark right after school. And then there's no time for winter fun.

If I thought winter in Kersville was going to be any different, boy, was I wrong.

Big-time!

See, that's me, Andres Miedoso, under all that snow. And that's my best friend, Desmond Cole, with the snowballs.

And that's the sleepwalking snowman. Yeah, you heard me right.

DESMOND COLE

ANDRES MIEDOSO

How did we end up here? Well, like I said, winter is *weird*!

Let me start at the beginning.

OUR SNOWY NIGHTMARE

CHAPTER TWO

A SNOWMAN PROBLEM

It was a perfect winter day. Desmond and I were in his garage, also known as the Ghost Patrol office.

I took a sip of hot chocolate and slurped down one of the warm, melty marshmallows. It tasted ooey-gooey and hot . . . just the way I like it.

"What's that?" I asked, pointing to one of the strange gadgets hanging on his wall.

"It's the Goblin Detector 3000," Desmond said. "But it doesn't work."

My hands started to shake. "G-goblin detector?" I asked.

Desmond smiled. "When I  get it to work, we'll be able to find goblins anywhere!"

He was excited about this. Me? I was happy living a goblin-free life!

A knock on the door made me jump.

"Looks like we have a customer!" Desmond said as he opened the door.

A bunch of snow and cold air blew inside. So did a kid, wrapped from head to toe in heavy winter gear.

"Welcome to the Ghost Patrol," Desmond said to the kid.

All we heard was a muffled grunt as the kid unwrapped a super-long scarf.

Underneath the pile of clothes was a boy. I didn't know him, but I had seen him around school.

"My name is Carter James," he said with a scared look in his eyes. "I have a problem."

"Is it a monster problem?" asked Desmond.

Carter shook his head. "No."

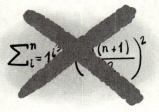

"Is it a ghost problem?" Desmond asked.

"No," Carter said.

I leaned forward and asked, "Is it a *math* problem?"

"No," Carter said.

Why can't anyone ever come here with a math problem? I thought. That  was something I could actually handle. Plus, math was never scary!

Desmond sat behind his desk. "Tell us what kind of problem you have, Carter."

The kid looked over his shoulder, like he was making sure we were alone. "It's a *snowman* problem," he whispered. "You see, I built a snow-man in my yard yesterday. But when I woke up this morning, my snowman was gone."

"That's easy to solve," Desmond said. "It snowed so much last night, your snowman got covered up."

"Nope," Carter said. "That's not what happened."

"Maybe some other kids knocked it down," I guessed.

"Y-you don't understand," Carter said with a shaky voice. "I f-found the snowman."

Now I was getting a little bit nervous. Something about his story was creeping me out.

"Well, then, the mystery's solved!" I said. "Sounds like you don't need us."

"I need your help," Carter pleaded.

"My snowman moved to another yard . . . all by itself. Then it vanished. I don't know where it is!"

A walking snowman?

That was all Desmond needed to hear. The Ghost Patrol had a new case!

CHAPTER THREE

TOASTY TOES

Back at my house, I prepared for the snowman mystery.

The secret to battling the freezing cold is wearing layers of clothes. I put on my favorite red sweater, then my red vest, then the blue scarf and hat my mom knitted for me.

Last, but not least, I put on my winter boots. I loved them! They were the thickest, furriest, warmest boots I had ever worn. No matter how slushy and cold it was outside, my toes were always dry and toasty!

The doorbell rang. Of course it was Desmond. He was wearing his Ghost Patrol backpack. That meant he was on the case.

When Desmond stepped inside, he stopped in his tracks and stared at me.

"What?" I asked him. What could take away Desmond's power of speech? It had to be something *big*!

"What's wrong?" I asked again. "Come on, Desmond. Talk to me, man. This isn't funny."

I started to tremble. Was there something behind me? A monster? A mummy? *A goblin?*

I swallowed hard and waited for Desmond's answer, but he just kept staring.

Just then Zax floated into the room through the wall. "Hey, guys," he said. But then he stopped talking and stared at me too. His ghost mouth dropped all the way to the ground!

"Not you, too, Zax!" I screamed. My heart was thumping. "What is everybody staring at?"

Finally, Desmond and Zax looked at each other and burst out laughing.

Zax said, "It's your boots, Andres!"

"Yeah," Desmond said. "They're
so . . . furry. Did you steal them from
Bigfoot? Or wrestle them away from
a bear?"

Zax nodded as he giggled. "Are they still alive?"

"You guys are *the worst*!" I said as my heart slowed to its normal speed. "We'll see who's laughing when my feet are warm and your feet are freezing!"

Zax cackled again. "Dude, I don't even have any feet!"

Okay, that made me laugh too. A lot. Maybe too much.

Desmond cleared his throat. "Are you ready?"

I nodded. It was time to find the missing snowman.

27

CHAPTER FOUR

SNOWBALL BULLY

Since Zax couldn't stop giggling every time he looked at my boots, Desmond and I decided to leave him at home. After all, we were on a serious mission. No giggling allowed!

Soon we were at Carter's house across from Kersville Park.

Carter yawned big and loud. "Sorry. I couldn't sleep last night." He walked across the yard and stopped near a tree. Desmond and I followed him. The spot was completely empty. "This is where I built the snowman."

Right away, Desmond opened his backpack and got to work. A few minutes later, he had set up some flags and tied yellow tape around that part of the yard. Desmond called it "the Ghost Patrol scene." He really took his job seriously.

Finally, Desmond said, "Carter, tell me about your snowman."

Carter pulled a slip of paper out of his pocket. "Here—I wrote down all the details."

Desmond nodded. I could tell he liked this Carter kid.

After reading the notes, Desmond searched the Ghost Patrol scene, looking for clues. Then he dropped to his knees and pulled out a . . . *ruler*? Desmond Cole had a ton of gadgets in his backpack. Why would he need a ruler of all things?

"Do you see what I see?" Desmond asked, measuring the snow. "Look at these!"

I bent down. When I looked closely, I could see there were foot-prints. They were plain with no boot treads or anything. They looked kind of fluffy, too.

Whoever moved the snowman must have been lighter than air!

Suddenly something freezing cold hit my head. "Aargh!" I screamed. "What was that?"

THUD! It hit me again, but this time I knew what it was: *a snowball.*

"Hey!" I yelled, looking around. "That's not cool."

Another snowball hit me on the
arm. I ducked down.

"Oh no!" Desmond hollered. "It's Cindy Lee! Run for it!"

Across the street, I saw a little girl with an armful of snowballs pop out from behind a tree. And just like an automatic pitching machine, she threw those snowballs at us fast and *hard*!

No one had to tell me twice. I ran away. "Who is Cindy Lee?"

"She's the neighborhood snowball bully," said Desmond. "Nobody can win a snowball fight against her. She never misses, and you never see her coming."

We reached the back of Carter's house and everyone stopped to catch their breath.

"Just once," Carter huffed, "I'd love to win a snowball fight against Cindy Lee."

That wouldn't be easy. She hit me with so many snowballs that I looked like a snowman. But thanks to my boots, my toes were still super toasty!

CHAPTER FIVE

THE SNOWDRIFT

We waited, silent and still, listening for signs of the snowball bully. But all we heard was nothing. It was a perfectly quiet winter day.

We peeked our heads out and stared at the park across the street. Cindy Lee was gone.

Desmond waved a plan to us with
his hands: He wanted us to split up
and check behind all the trees in the
park for the missing snowman.

I had a hand signal of my own. It meant *Let's go home and have a cup of hot chocolate!* Unfortunately, nobody understood my signal.

So, we split up and searched the park. Desmond went one way, and Carter went the other. Before I knew it, I was all by myself.

Warm feet or not, I didn't like being alone. Especially when I was looking for someone I didn't really want to find.

Sure, there were other kids and parents in the park, but none of them knew that a snowball bully was on the loose.

I ducked from one tree to the other, expecting Cindy Lee to jump out any second. But I didn't find her anywhere. I started to relax.

That was when a kid on a sled flew by me at top speed. He was moving so fast that I had to jump out of his way. I landed in a huge snowdrift.

"Ow," I moaned, lying there. "That hurt."

Leaning against the snowdrift, I had an idea. I could use this as a fort in case Cindy Lee came back!

I started making snowballs and putting them in a pile. Then I noticed something very weird about my winter fort. It had two huge, snowy feet. Looking up, I saw buttons, a long red scarf, and a black hat.

I stood up, forgetting all about Cindy Lee, and stared at my fort. It had a face . . . with a carrot nose and scary teeth!

I almost screamed. This wasn't a snowdrift. This was the biggest snowman I had ever seen!

It looked so creepy that I waved my arms in front of it to make sure it wasn't alive. The snowman didn't move, but this was Kersville. Almost everything here was haunted. So I did the most logical thing I could think of: I climbed onto the snowman and tried to pull off its carrot nose. I tugged and tugged, but it was frozen in tight.

"Hey, Desmond and Carter!" I yelled. "Come here!"

A few seconds later, Desmond came over alone. "It's just me.

Carter was tired so he went home to get some sleep—Whoa! That's a big snowman. Are you trying to climb to the top?"

CHAPTER SIX

FRIGHTFUL WEATHER

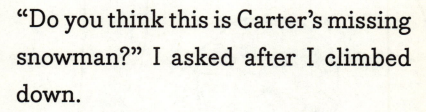

"Do you think this is Carter's missing snowman?" I asked after I climbed down.

Desmond walked around and pulled out the paper that Carter had given him. "There's only one way to find out. We will follow this list."

That made sense to me.

"Are there three buttons?" asked Desmond.

"Check," I said. This snowman had three buttons.

"And a red scarf?"

"Check."

"And a black—"

But before Desmond could finish talking, we heard a strange noise. It sounded like a low groan.

"What was that?" I asked.

Desmond shrugged. "Dunno."

Then we heard it again. But it wasn't a groan. It was a . . . *yawn*?

And it came from the snowman.

The creature lifted its arms high into the air and yawned again.

"The snowman is waking up!" Desmond screamed. "Come on!"

Desmond ran, but I was too scared to move. I was frozen. Well, everything except my toasty toes, but you already knew that.

"Andres," Desmond yelled. "Move!"

The snowman looked down at me and smiled with its scary, jagged teeth. Then it leaned over and let out a sound that came from deep inside all that snow.

It was a *growl*!

I could definitely run then!

The snowman stumbled after us with its arms outstretched. It was trying to snatch us!

Or was it trying to eat us?

Either way, I didn't want to find out.

Desmond and I ran
across the park.
We jumped over
kids on sleds.

We slid under
teens practicing on
their snowboards.

We swooped along the
cross-country trails,
weaving in between
skiers.

Nothing was going to stop us!
Nothing . . . until *whack*!

A snowball hit the side of my face.
Cindy Lee was back!

Whack! Whack!

"Ow!" Desmond and I screamed
as snowballs crashed all around us.

Cindy Lee was hiding behind a tree, and she had a pile of snowballs beside her! We were trapped! If we ran one way, we'd be attacked by a snowball bully. But if we ran the other way, we'd be eaten by a snow-man monster.

Desmond and I nodded at each other. There was only one thing to do. We ran toward Cindy Lee!

And nobody could have been more surprised than Cindy Lee herself. She pelted us with snowballs until she saw the overgrown snowman chasing us. Her eyes widened bigger than big, and before we knew it, all three of us were running from the snowman *together*.

Actually, Cindy Lee was way faster than we were. She was gone in a flash.

Me on the other hand? I slipped and tumbled into the snow. Hard.

Luckily, we were at the top of an icy hill, and I slid down it on my back.

"Great idea!" Desmond called as he leaped into the air headfirst. He slid down the hill on his belly and caught up to me.

Then we glided onto the crowded ice rink at the bottom of the hill. We kept sliding until we crashed right into a heating lamp.

I closed my eyes, waiting to be grabbed by that snowman. But nothing happened.

So I opened my eyes just in time to see the snowman. It was still at the top of the hill, looking down at us. Its stare sent shivers through my body.

But it didn't come after us anymore. Instead, it turned around and walked back into the woods.

CHAPTER SEVEN

WAKE UP

For the first time ever, Desmond Cole didn't chase after a creepy monster. "Let's go back to Carter's house to check out the Ghost Patrol scene," was all he said.

On the way there, I kept checking for that snowman.

73

I was still in shock. *Did a snow-man just come to life and chase us?* It was too crazy to be real.

The good thing was that the snow-man wasn't following us anymore. Plus, Cindy Lee was scared away. We were safe . . . for now.

Back at the Ghost Patrol scene, Desmond studied the area inside the yellow tape even more carefully now. "I must have missed something," he told me.

I sniffled. Being pelted with snowballs and chased in the cold air had
given me a runny nose. I needed a
tissue. *Fast!*

"I'll be right back," I said as I ran
to Carter's front door.

After a few knocks,
Carter answered, still
looking super sleepy.
I must have woken
him.

"Did you solve the
case yet?" he asked.

"No, not yet, but we found your
snowman," I said.

I could feel my snot turning into an icicle. "Do you have a tissue?"

"Sure. Yeah. Come in," Carter said. "There are tissues in the kitchen."

He went to get them, and while he was gone, I looked outside the window. Desmond was walking around with a flashlight strapped to his head.

He was carrying a new gadget, something I had never seen before. This was a strange one. It was a box that glowed, and it had a bunch of antennas pointing in different directions. Every few seconds, it changed color.

Now what was that?

Then something else caught my eye. The branches in the trees next to Carter's house were shaking, and a bunch of squirrels darted into the yard. As the furry critters passed Desmond, a white blob slipped out into the light.

It was the snowman!

Desmond was so focused on that glowing gadget that he didn't even know the snowman was there.

"Look out!" I yelled. But there was no way he could hear me from inside the house. I had to think fast!

That was when I got an idea. If I splashed that snowman with hot water, it would be melt-ville for that giant snowball for sure.

"Carter!" I yelled as I raced down the hall. "I need a thermos!"

In the kitchen, I found Carter completely asleep at the table. "Wake
up," I said, shaking him. "I need a
thermos. I have to melt your snowman. Fast!"

But I couldn't wait for Carter to
wake up. I looked around the kitchen,
found a few on my own, and filled
them with hot water.

As I ran back outside, I could hear Carter waking up. "What's going on?" he muttered. "Andres, wait!"

But I wasn't going to wait. I had to save Desmond!

Except when I opened the front door and ran into the yard, the snow-man was gone.

Desmond looked up from his weird device, which was glowing orange. He pointed to the thermoses. "Did you make me some tea?"

"Huh?" I asked. I was too busy searching the yard. "The snowman was here just a minute ago."

Desmond said, "I didn't see any-thing."

I wondered if it could have been all in my imagination, but the evidence was right there: giant footprints in the snow.

"Desmond, look!" I said, pointing. "See! The snowman *was* here!"

That was when Carter came outside and walked sleepily across the snow.

"Guys," he said, rubbing his eyes. "I just had the *weirdest* dream."

CHAPTER EIGHT

THUMPETY-THUMP-THUMP

Carter made us come back inside on account of he wasn't wearing his shoes. We went to his room. It was covered in posters of snowboarders and skiers and speed skaters. He even had a sled on the wall next to posters of igloos and . . . snowmen!

"Wow," I said. "You really love winter, don't you?"

"Oh yeah," Carter said, smiling. "It's my favorite season."

"Never mind that," Desmond said impatiently. "Put on your shoes and tell us about your dream so we can go find that snowman."

"You were in it, Desmond," Carter said. "And so were you, Andres. It was so strange. In the dream, I was chas-ing both of you when all of a sudden, we were all snowball-attacked by Cindy Lee. But for some reason, I didn't run away from her. I stood up to her. And *she* ran away from *me*! Weird, right?"

"Wait," I said. "That happened in real life. Only you weren't the one chasing us. The snowman was! You were dreaming something that really happened."

"That's impossible," Desmond said.

"As impossible as ghosts, monsters, and zombies?" I asked, because I had seen it all in Kersville! "I might know what's going on here," I said. "Have you ever heard of a golem?"

Both Desmond and Carter shook their heads.

"There is a golem in one of my video games," I told them. "You see, golems are these creatures that are made out of, like, mud or clay. But then they come to life and have to do whatever the person who made them wants them to do."

"I don't get it," Desmond said. "The snowman is made of snow, not mud or clay."

"Maybe snow works the same way," I suggested.

Carter yawned. "Do you think I'm controlling the snowman?"

I shrugged. "Maybe? I don't know how it all works. This is just a guess."

Desmond still looked confused. "Why would Carter make the snowman chase after us?"

This was the first time I knew something Desmond didn't. "Golems aren't all that smart," I explained.

"They do what you want, but they like to do things their own way."

Desmond and Carter still looked like they didn't understand.

So I continued talking. "Carter needed us to help him with his prob-lem," I said. "Maybe the snowman thought it needed to *catch* us!"

Carter shook his head and yawned again. "But I didn't tell the snowman to do anything! I promise. You've been with me this whole time. And I wasn't even around to see the snowman."

That got me thinking. Every time we saw the snowman come to life, Carter was home . . . asleep.

"That's it!" I said, clapping my hands. "The snowman is sleepwalking! And, Carter, you're controlling it when you sleep. That's why you've been having such weird dreams."

Finally, Desmond nodded and turned to Carter. "Yes! Andres is right. Let's see what happens if you take a nap for a little while."

"I *am* pretty sleepy," Carter said. "I'll just lie down for a few minutes."

He climbed into his bed, and he was fast asleep in no time.

Desmond and I stood there, not sure what to expect. A few seconds later, we heard something from downstairs. **THUMPETY-THUMP-THUMP!**

The sound was getting closer.

And closer.

THUMPETY-THUMP-THUMP!

Suddenly, Carter's bedroom door swung open.

The sleepwalking snowman had found us!

97

CHAPTER NINE

CATCH ME IF YOU CAN

I heard a scream. And then another. And then another! But of course, it was only me screaming.

The snowman blocked the whole doorway. It was impossible to escape.

Desmond yelled, "Let's wake up Carter and stop him from dreaming!"

We shook Carter, but it was no use. That kid could sleep!

The snowman entered the room, creeping closer and closer.

I swallowed hard. "Remember, Carter doesn't want to hurt us, so the snowman won't hurt us."

Then the snowman launched a snowball that hit me square in the face.

Splat!

Desmond cleared his throat. "I thought it didn't want to hurt us."

"Maybe I was wrong," I said as the snowman loomed over us with its arms outstretched. "Haven't you ever been wrong before?"

I screamed again and waited for the snowman to grab us.

But before that could happen, Desmond grabbed the sled from Carter's wall.

"Get behind me," Desmond said, holding the sled in front of us like a shield.

The snowman pelted the sled with snowballs.

"Let's get out of here!" Desmond cried.

We moved around the snowman, then bolted out of the room, down the stairs, and through the front door at top speed. As soon as we hit the yard, we both hopped onto the sled. We had to get away from there!

Only we didn't get far.

In a flash, the snowman jumped out of Carter's bedroom window and landed right in front of us. It was quick for a pile of snow!

"Hold on tight," Desmond said, swerving around the frozen beast.

The sled was fast, but the snowman was faster. *Much* faster! He was
so fast that it seemed to be skating
on the snow!

The snowman reached out to grab
me, but it ended up with just a piece
of my scarf. "Let go!" I screamed.
No way was I going to give up the
scarf my mom made for me!

So I tugged it back and almost fell off the sled. Desmond held me as we picked up speed.

"Where are we going?" I asked Desmond, wiping the snow from my eyes.

"We need to find Cindy Lee," he said. "I have a plan."

Desmond Cole *always* had a plan!

We flew into the park, weaving in and out of the trees. Desmond and I looked back and saw that the snowman was still chasing us.

"What's the plan?" I asked as we hit a hill and slid down it.

"Remember when Carter said he always wanted to win a snowball fight against Cindy Lee?" Desmond asked. "Well, I bet if the snowman sees Cindy Lee, it will stop chasing us and fight with her!"

That was a great idea . . . with only one problem. *We* didn't find Cindy Lee. Cindy Lee found *us*! Which meant we were stuck between a snowball bully and a sleepwalking snowman again!

Thwack!

"Owww!" I screamed as Cindy Lee bombarded us with snowballs. That girl had some kind of aim.

Luckily, Desmond's plan worked.

When the sleepwalking snowman saw Cindy Lee, it froze. What came next was the most epic snowball fight in history.

It was so awesome that Desmond and I stopped sledding so we could watch.

At first, the snowman had the upper hand, but then Cindy Lee came roaring back. As the snowballs hurled across the park, Desmond whispered to me, "Andres, give me your boots."

"Are you really going to make fun of my boots at a time like this?" I snapped.

"No way," Desmond said. "We need your boots now more than ever. Please?"

I sighed, then I took off my boots and handed them over to him. My dry, warm toes were now super cold and wet. This new idea had better be a good one.

Desmond snuck over behind the snowman. There was no way the creature was going to notice him. It was too busy flinging snowballs at Cindy Lee.

Then Desmond set my boots on the ground.

As the snowman dodged the snow-balls, it stepped into my boots, and it must have been like stepping into the sun.

That snowman started to sweat like crazy. Then I realized that it wasn't sweating.
It was *melting*!

It didn't take long before the snowman was nothing more than a large
puddle.

Cindy Lee stopped throwing snowballs as I ran over to get my boots.
Oof! Gross! They smelled like wet
dog.

My poor, toasty boots were ruined,
but the sleepwalking snowman case
was solved!

CHAPTER TEN

MELT AWAY

It turns out that all Carter needed was a good night's sleep. His tired grumpiness had turned the snowman into a grumpy golem. But after some rest, Carter was able to build a new, nicer snowman. I know, it sounds crazy. Why build *another* snowman?

Well, because golems can be useful. While the whole town was asleep, Carter had his snowman build a perfect winter park for everyone to enjoy.

We called it the Kersville Winter Wonderland, and it had everything: an ice castle with ice slides, a hot chocolate fountain, an igloo bouncy house, and an icicle cave. There were even lanes for sledding races around the whole place.

Plus, there were forts that were filled with round, fluffy snowballs for snowball fights. They were perfect for throwing. It almost felt good to get hit with one . . . almost.

It was hard to believe that Carter created all of this in his sleep. Talk about wild dreams!

No one knew where the snow forts came from, but no one cared. Now people come from all over to visit Kersville's famous Winter Wonderland—but they have no idea it's a park that was built by a snowman!

Like I said before, winter is *weird*, but I think that's what makes it *the best!*